Bound by *Illness*
FREED *by* GRACE

Dear Dana

Thank you for all
your excellent care
while at Marlton Rehab.
I hope you enjoy the
book

With gratitude,
Maureen.

Bound by Illness
FREED by GRACE

Maureen Brady

Bound by Illness, Freed by Grace

First printing, 2014

Copyright © 2014 by Maureen Brady

Cover art copyright © by Andrew Gioulis
Cover photograph copyright © by Andrew Gioulis
Book design by Andrew Gioulis

Published by: KFR Communications, LLC

ISBN-13: 978-1494405830
ISBN-10: 1494405830

Printed in the United States of America

www.kfrcommunications.com

This book is dedicated to:

My cousin, Mary Gilbert Davis

My best friend, Eric Smith

My H (Hannah Gilbert, you are my heart)

To the strength and courage of:

Jeanette Gilbert

Debbie Seddon Mingo

Devon L. Wall, (my baby girl)

You know pain and you know victory!

In memory of:

Karen Riley and Benjamin Jon Siegel

Acknowledgements

Pastor Eric Hoheisel, Senior Pastor from Oaklyn Baptist Church in Oaklyn, NJ, who provided unending spiritual support.

Robyn Selvin who edited the first draft of this manuscript: I thank from the bottom of my heart for believing in me.

My Editor, Michelle Canales for all your support and hard work on this manuscript.

My sisters in Christ, Jennifer Basset and Cassandra Ulrich who pushed and encouraged me with great patience, support and feedback.

Primary Physician, Dr. Toby Sobel for being with me through all these years and caring for my medical needs.

Rebecca Golden, Physical Therapist, Penn Fitness and Therapy, Cherry Hill, NJ

Kathy Liddie, Occupational Therapist, Virtua In Motion Rehabilitation Department, Voorhees, NJ

The Deaf Ministry from Victory Assembly of God church in Centerton, NJ, who transported me, pushed me up and down hills and around in my wheelchair until I felt human again. I love you all so dearly.

Debbie Slone and Penny N. from Rest Ministries who together helped title the book.

Several members from Facebook's Chronic Pain Information page for making topic suggestions that were used in the book, including Elizabeth Mizioch-Crawford, Daniel Grome, and Ellen Perles-Silvia.

Jennasset Photopraphy, thank you for the head shot.

Pastor Eric Hoheisel, Jennifer Basset, Nancy and Steve Bellik, John and Wendy Butler, Dee Clark, Mary and Ronnie Davis, Julie Doerrmann, Tony Garnett. Pete and Jeanette Gilbert, Paul and Tammy Gilbert, Theresa Gilbert, Hannah Gilbert, Kathy Earp, Robyn Selvin, Eric Smith and the congregation from Oaklyn Baptist Church and Victory Assembly of God Church (as well as members of my family in Cape Town and Australia) and all the wonderful people from Rest Ministires who were my prayer warriors throughout this process.

All of you who have prayed me through many situations over the many years, you have my undying gratitude.

To Francis Chan, Mary DeMuth, Joyce Meyers, Andy Stanley and Joni Eareckson Tada whose books have taught me and inspired me beyond measure.

Most of all, to my Lord and Savior, Jesus Christ, whose Holy Spirit lead me to write this book. May all the glory go to Him.

Table of Contents

Foreword

As human beings, we can empathize with anyone that suffers with pain. We have all suffered from pain at some point in our lives. Some folk's experience with pain has been minimal, while others have experienced lengthy, debilitating episodes of pain.

Think back to a time that you, or a loved one, experienced a physical trauma, like surgery or an accident. The patient knows that the days, weeks, or possibly months ahead will be difficult. There is a period of recovery, pain medication, and maybe physical therapy, and then, healing occurs. In time, the injury heals, and the person resumes his/her regular activities with little consequence. It is never a pleasant experience, but an individual with acute pain knows that the pain is temporary, and will subside, and there will be resolve.

Now imagine that the same scenario of a sudden accident, or surgery, or onset of an illness occurs. The patient naturally expects things to be difficult for a while, and performs all of the healing measures he/she is told to do by the doctor. The patient takes his/her medication, completes his/her therapy, and follows all the instructions given by medical personnel, yet the pain continues, and increases at times, rather than dissipates as expected.

Suddenly, there is no end to the sharp, stabbing, burning, aching, throbbing pain this person is experiencing. Our natural reaction is to want the intense discomfort, and pain, to cease as soon as possible, so we would be willing to do what we can to make that happen. Chronic pain controls a person's life when no amount of therapy, medication, surgery, or other treatments, improve the painful symptoms.

Additionally, the ravishing effects of chronic pain cause a great deal of loss. There is a loss of independence, a loss of identity, and a huge financial loss that is often not considered. Folks with prolonged chronic pain, often feel like the shell of the person they used to be before the onset of pain.

Emotionally, a person who experiences chronic pain will also experience depression and hopelessness, frustration, loneliness, anger and fear. It is hard to find other folks who understand these emotions. People with chronic pain are often misunderstood by their family, friends, colleagues, and even their physicians.

But, an individual with acute pain knows that the pain is temporary, and will subside, and there will be resolve.

CHAPTER I

The Many Faces of Chronic Pain

I became aware of the soothing element of Yukon Jack whiskey.

"*Oh yes, everything is fine. Lovely. No problem.*" Trying to push myself through a day of pain is exhausting, especially when my body is screaming in rebellion. Trying to pretend the pain doesn't exist for the sake of others around me can exacerbate the problem.

I often consumed a great deal of alcohol because of the constant pain. I was regularly drinking 1.5 liter bottles of wine every few days. When my cleaning woman came, there were 9 or 10 empty bottles of wine piled up in my small kitchen. During this time, I discovered that a little bit of Yukon Jack went a long way. I had a walker that had a basket under the seat; my neighbors used to call it my traveling bar. I always had a supply of alcohol to keep me as numb as possible.

I had resorted to 'self- medicating.'

"*Happy face, Maureen, c'mon, smile, you can do it. You can make it. Laugh so they won't know. Laugh instead of crying. I can't let them know how miserable I am.*" I remember thinking, if they only knew the real extent of my pain, they would not think that I am complaining too much. I wished that those who looked at me with accusing eyes could be in my body for one week.

For years, just making it through an entire day at work was a great accomplishment. I recognized that God knew what I was going through, and that was all that mattered. If I dared try and do anything extra, shame on me. I knew that I was taking a risk going out with a friend, or stopping at the store. I would have to expend more energy and pretend that all could be done without consequence.

I desperately wanted a life. I held on tightly, but the act of simply trying to get to a destination, was a battle in itself. It took a great deal of calculating, whether or not I could make it where I needed to go: *Did I have the energy? Would it be populated that time of day? Did I have enough time to get there and back? Could I even get out of the chair I was sitting in by myself?* I would labouringly walk step-by-step using my cane, always looking at my feet, because I was afraid I might fall. It felt like I was running a marathon just to get to my car. I would be drenched in sweat just starting out.

Being out of my own environment was stressful. What made things worse was an Academy Award-worthy performance: pretending that I was managing fine. It was draining.

I remember having dinner with friends, and wondering if I was going to make it to my car afterwards. After the kiss, wave, and smile, I would start my car and the tears erupt. Once home, and on several occasions, I had to call my neighbor to help me get from the car to my apartment. I didn't know if my legs would take me there. The pain was excruciating, and the stress of trying to get to my apartment was overwhelming.

This is when I would pray a very simple prayer that I still pray today: *Help me, Lord. Help me, Father. Guide my steps, Jesus. I don't know if I can do this, but You do. With Your help, I will make it. Thank you, Lord. Thank you.*

I no longer feel the need to fake it. I am way past that now. Each step is labored and obviously difficult. I no longer have to collapse from exhaustion after pretending that I'm okay. What a relief.

Many people who experience chronic pain might need a cane, or a walker, or even a wheelchair to get around. It should be enough of a clue that a legitimate physical problem exists. Their credibility should not be challenged. There are countless others—diagnosed with conditions such as Fibromyalgia/Chronic Fatigue Syndrome,

Lymphedema, and Chronic Regional Pain Syndrome/Reflex Sympathetic Dystrophy—their pain cannot be seen outwardly. The result: Their condition is often misdiagnosed and misunderstood. Moreover, said folks with daily chronic pain—and with a cause remaining invisible—often suffer an additional consequence: Their pain is often doubted by their family, friends, and colleagues, and, sometimes even their physicians. This can cause more stress and, in turn, more physical and emotional pain.

Chronic pain can be confusing. For most of us, there are no absolutes. Situations can change from minute-to-minute. We can be happily walking and visiting with friends, one minute, and, the next minute, we are riddled with pain and may need to lie down. What we could do easily in the morning we cannot achieve, or even feign, at all in the afternoon. This is very frustrating for everybody involved. Loved ones may want to know how they can help. Sometimes we can't tell them because of the ever-changing facet of the pain. Well-meaning relatives, friends, and employers find it confusing that we can perform an activity one day, and not the next. Ergo, many comments are made out of ignorance.

Someone may say, "I saw you do this before, why can't you do it now?" Or, "Oh, c'mon, try a little harder, push yourself. I know you can do it." My personal favorite is, "You have to start to get out more often. It will make you feel better. Sitting around at home isn't helping. Do something instead of thinking about how badly you feel."

Unfortunately, people don't understand how much it takes to recover from even a short event. We do as much as we can, at any given moment, often pushing ourselves, and pay with an increase in pain or fatigue later. This is one of the reasons that many chronic pain sufferers prefer to keep their suffering private.

My best friend was constantly nagging me about reading. I did not have words to explain to her that I could not read effectively during that time. Clearly, I was physically able to read, however, I had no interest in reading at all. I was not capable of retaining the information due, in part, to my medication and a certain depression I was experiencing. She would go on these tangents, or perhaps verbal dissertations, about the negative effects of television, and insisted that I needed to stimulate my mind. It was a fruitless task trying to explain to her that this conversation was adding to my already mounting anxiety.

Chronic pain sufferers come to understand that what works for one might not work for another. We often must sit through snake-oil stories about what worked for so-and-sos', Great Aunt Tilly; a woman who had a condition similar to ours one-hundred years ago. Most of us nod, and listen, and try not to be rude. The reality is that, by necessity, the majority of us are fully aware of the treatments available for our given condition. We have tried many of these remedies. In some instances, some of these new "cures" have increased our pain or has resulted in sheer frustration. If a legitimate cure that worked somehow manifested into existence, most of us would already be aware of the treatment. Part of working with your physician is learning how to discuss viable options and alternatives.

I have to laugh at the number of people that continue to point out the impact my weight has on my health. First of all, I am well aware that being overweight can make a condition go from bad to worse. Most doctors, physical therapists, and specialists also point this out. Some of us, who are heavy and have a chronic illness, know that people blame the illness on our weight. For the most part, the two are in no way connected. The immobility, a result of the chronic pain, causes us to have a difficult time with our weight. Others have weight issues, or just fluctuations, caused from various medications that their doctors prescribe.

Using food as a mechanism to cope with depression, can be another factor causing weight gain. If chronic pain resulted from merely being overweight, thin people suffering with pain would not exist.

Subsequently, chronic pain and depression seem to go hand-in-hand. It is not our intention to appear morbid or be constantly miserable. We also do not want to seem anti-social. I often worry about people rolling their eyes in disbelief, on the other end of the telephone receiver, if I should start talking about yet another problem. Most of us try very hard to be as pleasant and polite as possible. We can't always fake it. Folks with chronic pain will try—the best they know how—to cope with a situation that is draining and depressing. Many of our days are filled with considerable discomfort and exhaustion.

Frustration naturally manifests when we go to physicians for help, and, after completing diagnostic testing, they tell us that they can't help because nothing appears to be wrong. Additionally, the doctor may suggest that the case is so complicated, that we just have to live with our circumstance. At times, there appears to be no hope, and no help, from the medical community. These conundrums affect the patients, and their friends and family, invested in recovery. Constantly seeking a solution to our health problems can be grueling and expensive. As a result, many have given up, and simply continue to seek ways to cope with their chromic illnesses.

However, we are so grateful for the help we receive from the people in our lives. I depended on friends and family, for almost everything, for several years. If I had a need, I would spend a great deal of time wondering *how* and *when* I was going to get what I needed. It caused anxiety. Sometimes I still might need help with shopping, and cleaning, and getting various errands done. It is the people in our lives who keep us going, be it a husband or wife, children, neighbors or friends, as well as members of our church family.

Many of us are left wondering, *where is God in these circumstances? If God is good, why would He allow such suffering? What could possibly be the point of this anyway?* Many folks turn away from God at this time. Things were not supposed to turn out like this; I've prayed for healing and nothing has happened. We can love what the Bible says about many things, and even about suffering and affliction, in theory. But, suddenly, we are living it and it takes on a new dimension. J.C. Ryle, the former bishop of Liverpool, ardently argues for the body and soul's sanctification through affliction:

> Affliction is one of God's medicines. By it He often teaches lessons which would be learned in no other way. By it He often draws souls away from sin and the world, which would otherwise have perished everlastingly. Health is a great blessing, but sanctified disease is a greater. Prosperity and worldly comfort, are what all naturally desire; but losses and crosses are far better for us, if they lead us to Christ. Thousands at the last day will testify with David, [Psalm 119:71] "It is good for me that I have been afflicted."

What do you mean it is good that I have been afflicted? That is madness. My entire life and the lives of my family are being affected. I was active in my community, and my church, doing work for God, and now I have major limitations to what I can do. I had to cut down my involvement with various activities in order to manage this pain. It is seemingly nonsensical to suggest that pain and illness can somehow benefit me. In turn, I am depressed and broke: both financially and spiritually. *What good can possibly come out of this?*

How dare I question God? How dare I complain? If this is what God's will is for me then I should just accept it. I know God has my best interest at heart, so I will just bear the pain on my own. If this is the life I was suddenly given, then I should be equipped to handle it; and I will with my head held high.

It takes a long time to recognize the benefits of sharing in Christ's suffering. Initially, it made no sense to me. I was not prepared for my life to take this turn in the road. I have many plans for my life, and when God changes those plans, I don't understand. I am often unprepared, and feel ill-equipped, to deal with the chaos that chronic illness brings. Many folks, myself included, waste their time by lamenting over their ill-fated pain. Or, many may use their pride to try and manage the situation devoid of God's help. It is natural to feel despair. In this situation, it's natural to be afraid of the future. The obstacles in our lives, at times, seem to be growing exponentially and we can't control it. To try and struggle through chronic illness, rather than accept it, seems like the right thing to do. If we give into it, it might be perceived as giving up. That is unacceptable.

Conversely, affliction that fills me with illness and sorrow, also brings me to a place before God that I would never know without it. I draw nearer to God out of necessity. My prayers become deeper, and my devotion becomes stronger. I now pour my soul before God; I learn to depend on God in a way I never imagined I could.

As I become more and more dependent on Him, I notice my own evolution to positive change. In order to survive the daily struggles that befall me, I find myself in Scripture and prayer from morning until night. I am conscious of the presence of the Lord God Almighty in my life.

I suddenly start to see God's grace and His strength in my weakness. I celebrate this transformation and thank God for this opportunity. Without all the illness, heartbreak, and grief I have experienced, I would never have grown to this point, spiritually. There is transformation.

CHAPTER 2

𝒟𝒩𝒜

Good timber does not grow with ease,
the stronger the wind, the stronger the tree.
—*John Marriott*

My parents were wed on February 16, 1952, in England. On the very day they were married, my mother realized she made a big mistake. In her efforts to look out for her family, she sacrificed herself. My mom initially figured that she would be able to help her family best if she married well, and if she eventually moved to the United States. So she did.

America was the land of opportunity and, in her mind, it would be the salvation of the Randal family. My father's family, the Bradys, treated my mother very well. They did not know what to expect when my father told them that he married a woman from South Africa (I think they pictured somebody who lived in a hut and had a bone in her nose). When my parents arrived in America, they had a completely furnished apartment waiting for them in Oaklyn, New Jersey.

The apartment was close to where my grandmother lived; that was a blessing for my mother while my father was traveling out of the country. Here in America, my mother easily made friends. People were attracted to her lovely accent, stunning good looks, and simply sincere disposition. She missed her family very much, but was content (until the next time my father came home).

It took my parents seven years before they could conceive a child. My mother had a tilted uterus. After a nasty fall on some ice, her uterus tilted back into the proper place, which, finally, allowed her to conceive a child. I was born on July 20, 1959. My mom was thirty-eight years old and my father was forty-nine. She was an over-protective worrier. My mother said she used to sit at the edge of my bed every night, and just stand guard over me. She wasn't sure exactly why she had to do it, but she just knew that she had to. It would be the same ritual, night after night, until she was sure that I would survive infancy.

My father was out of the country when I was born, and did not see me until I was six weeks old. He was not there to help my mother with the stress of being a new mom. She did it alone; that would be the pattern for the rest of her life.

In 1961, my parents moved from their quaint apartment in Oaklyn, to a three-bedroom house in Lindenwold, New Jersey. It was called a "Charm Home". My mom was thrilled to be both a homeowner and a mother. I was two years old at the time, and, even as a toddler, my mother or one of the neighbors, would catch me sneaking out the front gates, or running down the street. That is something that never, ever changed: The desire to run.

The neighbors in our town were very close, especially those on East Maple Avenue. We all knew each other, and stuck together through good and bad times. They helped each other raise their kids. If one of us did something wrong, the neighbor would yell at us before she told our mom. This was a common occurrence across the United States during the 1950s and 60s. The folks from the neigh-borhood often looked out for each other's children. I remember being mortified while walking home from the mall; I decided to hitch-hike and my mom's best friend, Mrs. Grace, picked me up. I knew I was in for it then.

The funny thing was that the kids also stuck together, especially when we got older. I was best- friends with another girl also named Maureen while in elementary school. Maureen was a year younger than me. People referred to Maureen and I as "little Maureen" and "big Maureen". Little Maureen and I did all the normal kid things. We ran behind the mosquito-exterminator-truck and are still alive to tell that story (who knows what chemicals came out of the back of that truck)? I can still smell that rancid odor, and I remember my eyes burning, but pressing forward with glee in the cloud of toxicity. We saved our pennies, walked to the corner store and bought candy cigarettes, and dots, and pixie sticks. Nothing excited us more than the sound of the Mr. Softee truck approaching our block. That was a serious, "beg the parents", moment in time. To this day, I still smile when I hear the same tune playing from the Mr. Softee trucks that drive down the street.

I remember when Maureen and I decorated our bikes with red, white, and blue streamers for the big Fourth of July parade that roared down the block behind ours. We would tape a balloon, or piece of cardboard, to the spokes of our wheels to simulate an engine-type sound. The noise would bring attention to us, so, if the balloon stayed inflated, it meant we were something special. It meant we were somehow gifted—or so we thought. I always lagged far behind the others, whether I was walking or riding my bike.

I hosted many pajama parties when I was a kid. I had at least ten friends show up with their sleeping bags and baby-doll pajamas. Mom would have lots snacks for us; we would sit with our legs crossed, in a circle, and tell jokes, and play games. The girls would squeal with delight while stretching across, over, and around the colored spheres of the Twister game board. Once and a while, a tear would shed after a pillow fight gone awry. Sometimes, we would even dress up like hula dancers, with grass skirts and fake leis around our necks, thinking we were Hawaii's answer to the Rockettes.

We would also throw in an occasional scary moment as we held hands and tried to conjure up the ghost of Mary Jane Joyce. None of us really knew who Mary Jane Joyce was. All we knew was that we were supposed to repeat her name while looking into the mirror, and then she would appear. It was thrilling, yet frightening, and we thought, "the scarier the better".

Eventually, the lights got turned off, and candles were lit, and my mom would enter our circle. All my friends would uncross their legs, and lay with both hands under their chins, with everybody's attention focused on my mother. Mom would start by explaining that she was born with "the veil" and what that meant. She would then proceed to tell ghost stories. Her shadow covered the wall behind her.

She spoke of a headless man in a suit. He sat, facing a window that she passed by, while she was coming down the fire escape. The horror intensified. My mom built suspense with each step ,or sequence of events. By the time she got to the last step she would whisper, "Later we found out that a man in that apartment was fixing his window when, 'CHOP!' Rumor has it, that his head was cut off when the window slipped and fell on his neck. The man's head rolled down the fire escape steps." She was very animated and used her best, soft-but-very-scary voices to describe what she saw, and how she ran after seeing that hideous sight that only she could witness.

Suddenly, girls thought that they could see the headless man's silhouette in every shadow. You could see the goose bumps forming. My friends' eyes got as big as saucers. Some of them looked frozen in place. Next, pillows were being hugged or girls were climbing into their sleeping bags. It was like clockwork; one girl would start crying, and then the next. Before I knew it, the cars of their parents were lined up outside of my house to pick up their frightened children. If I was lucky, I had maybe two friends left that slept over until the next morning. (Usually, it was because they fell asleep during my mother's scary stories.) At the next pajama party, the same children would come, and my mom would tell the same stories, and the same cars would come in the late night hours to pick up the same crying children.

❧

The Catholic Church we attended was right around the corner. Every morning at 7 am, every evening at 7 pm, and right before each Mass, the church bells would ring. That rich melodic tone will remain in my memory as, perhaps, the most magnificent sound ever. If I shut my eyes and just listen, I can still hear the bells of St. Lawrence —still soothing my soul.

I attended St. Lawrence Catholic School. It was only a block over from my home, which sat next to the church and the convent. As a child, I loved that my mother was so active at my school. My mom was considerably older than the other women that worked in the kitchen to make lunches on "pizza day". The other children loved my mother because they saw the twinkle in her eyes, and were fascinated with her foreign accent. Every year, for as long as I could remember, my mother worked the carnivals at St. Lawrence as well.

St. Lawrence Carnival was to die for. Every year in June, the Skelly carnival would pull into town. I would lose a night of sleep, the Saturday night before, as I listened, through my window, I could make out the clinking and clanking of assembly: the rides and booths were set up initially, followed by an even louder installment of the spinning wheels. Oh, how I would rush out the door for church that next morning; as I turned the corner, there it was, the yearly carnival! It was the most anticipated event of the year next to Christmas.

The time between Sunday and Monday seemed endless. We had our ride tickets purchased in advance, and piled onto the school grounds the minute the booths opened up. We put our quarters down on our lucky numbers trying to win our favorite stuffed animals. We tossed bean bags, flung plastic rings at bottles, and threw balls into small fish bowls. We students could be found stuffing our faces with cotton candy, funnel cake, and snow cones.

My favorite ride: The "Salt and Pepper Shakers". Oh, the thrill of being propelled forward in a metal cylinder cage-like enclosure. The ride mimicked the action of shaking a salt and pepper shaker, only you were *inside* the shaker. The next thing we knew, we were backwards, and upside down, and screaming louder than anybody else ever screamed. What a rush! A lot of the kids were afraid of the Salt and Pepper Shakers, but I wasn't one of them. I felt brave.

On some of his more sober days, my father took us on outings. He loved driving around Six Flags Great Adventure Safari. My dad had a passion for safari animals, especially giraffes. He went on a real

Safari while he was in South Africa, and he brought home two real safari suits: one was tan, and, the other, blue. Every week, without fail, my father wore one of his safari suits to church. His weekly tradition became known as the, "Sunday Safari". My dad enjoyed taking me to the Atco drive-in movies. I remember being thrilled to see, *The Jungle Book*, with my dad. He drove his white, 1966 Dodge Monaco. (My father was also known as, "Prince Vince of Monaco", because of that car).

I loved it when we approached our parking spot—there was that magical glide up the incline that left your car pointed at the screen—the excitement would mount as my dad reached for the box-shaped speaker and attached it to his car door window. Nothing was better than this! The anticipation would throw me over the edge. I don't know which was more exciting, being at the drive-in or being with my father?

Most perceived my mother as a loving, happy person. In reality, she had a wicked temper that was only seen by a few unlucky people. She often raged for hours if I did something that warranted her disapproval. Her eyes would bulge out of her face, and she would call me names like, "you big dummy", or she would tell me that I was ungrateful and stupid. She could also become extremely critical if I wore the wrong clothes or watched the wrong TV show. I never knew what would cause one of these moods and when it would strike. I never knew exactly what was going to set my mom off. I cannot deny that I was a tough child to raise; I undoubtedly gave my mother plenty of fuel to ignite her fierce anger.

If my father was home, the tension was much worse. If I even thought their voices might to escalate, I would get a knot in my stomach. When the shouting started, I would walk back and forth—pacing and grabbing my temples—I would hit myself on my head, as hard as I could, just to have a distraction. I would blast my radio, on full volume, but it never seemed to be able to drown out the screaming. *Can't the neighbors hear this?* I wondered. Sometimes, minutes felt like hours. *Where do I go? What do I do? How do I make this stop?*

Wow, she is so mean, I would think to myself. *Whoa, are you kidding me, did he really just say that?* I didn't want to listen. I didn't want to hear their words or feel their hate. But, it still crept up the walls, and through the vents, and into my being. Occasionally I would scream, "sssshhhhuuuuutttt! upppppp!", at the top of my lungs, but they never seemed to hear me. They were too busy cursing each other's very existence.

In a way, I felt bad for my mother. I was a very strong-willed child; I was very creative. She had me later in life. Moreover, I did not think the same way as the other children. I did not learn the way as other children. I was not thin or fashion conscious like my peers. My large size was unacceptable to my mother—she was beautiful and charming, to both men and women—she was deeply rooted in the art of being a female.

In contrast, I was rude, aggressive, and demanding. As an only child, I liked my space and solitude. As a result, my mother had an immensely hard time controlling me.

⁂

Our experiences in childhood often shape the people we become and determine how we deal with our challenges as adults. Part of having chronic pain involves depending on others.

The dynamics change when a chronic illness moves into the home. It now becomes a family illness. The family becomes affected by our limitations. Not only is there guilt about not being able to do what we could do before, there is also inherent guilt about being dependent on family members. This transition is a very difficult thing for most of us to accept.

We never want to feel like a burden to our loved ones. We might really want a cup of coffee, or extra blanket, but may NEVER ask for something so simple because we feel it is not a necessity. Conversely, executing those tasks ourselves is not worth the pain or loss of energy it will cause. We get used to doing without the simple things in life that we enjoy. Most of our family, or friends, would be willing to make us a cup of tea, locate the remote to change the television channel, add more cream to our coffee, or grab us a sweater, if we would only ask. They are simple things; they can help.

Don't hesitate to ask your spouse or children to assist you. Your family, or neighbors, might indeed feel helpless to alleviate your discomfort. In my experience, helping with small tasks makes them feel like they are helping, and they are.

Rides to the doctor, shopping, laundry, and house cleaning might take a little more creativity to get accomplished. Since I was unable to perform these tasks myself, I decided to divide them up so that everything wouldn't fall on one person. I relied on family, friends, church family, neighbors and former colleagues. That idea worked well for a while.

We all don't have a big Italian family with twenty people willing to lend a hand. In fact, I am an only child, and I live alone in an apartment. My church friends did as much they could to assist me. I have four cousins. Only one, my cousin Mary, and her two sons (I call them my nephews) took the brunt of the "helper" role. I believe Mary will be wearing some serious crowns in glory; I'll tell you that much. She was always there to serve me, and never complained once. She never made me feel badly about anything. I tell her often that I would never have made it through that time without her. I would probably be living in assisted living or worse. She is indeed, my hero.

CHAPTER 3

Children with Chronic Pain

In my opinion children who suffer with chronic pain often become emotionally distressed and feel more vulnerable. I know I did as a child. Even the parents of chronically ill children experience amplified levels of depression and anxiety that often spill over into other areas of their lives: namely, financial difficulties and heightened marital problems. Often, parents of a chronically ill child must overlook their own grief and anguish in order to advocate for their child. Similarly, siblings of those children, with chronic pain, can suffer a profound affect due to their sibling's illness. The attention of the parents, and other family members, may become concentrated on the child who is ill, therefore, the other siblings in the home may feel largely ignored.

In the area of pain management, there is, at times, a lack of pediatric care; this increases the possibility of children being left untreated until they become adults with chronic pain. Children cannot always verbalize the feeling of pain or discomfort they are experiencing. They depend on their parents, or the other significant people in their lives, to protect them and keep them safe from harm. For the most part, it is the family members, or the family physician, that first notice a physical problem. Most parents can identify that something is wrong when they notice that one child is developing differently than their other children. However, sometimes this requires careful observation.

It is easy to blame discomfort or lack of physical activity on a child's weight gain. Whether or not the pain comes from being obese, or the obesity comes from being in pain, a child's complaints should not be ignored. Some chronic illnesses are mistaken for growing pains. Making a diagnosis, and receiving treatment in childhood, can majorly affect how a person functions in adulthood.

My mother loved me dearly. I was her only child and her baby girl. She chose to concentrate her efforts on weight management. Her way of dealing with said problem was to embarrass it out of me. Unfortunately, it didn't work, and instead caused self-esteem problems that carried on into adulthood. As a child, I kept many things to myself because I did not want to disappoint my mother. It never occurred to my mom that I might have a physical ailment. I was thirteen years old when a blood test revealed hypothyroidism; it is also known as an under-active thyroid. This is what caused me to be tired and sluggish during my younger years. It also contributed to the weight gain. I was put on medication and immediately lost weight. Although the "fat and lazy" did seem to apply, that was how my mother verbalized symptoms of a legitimate physical problem before she knew there was one. I put no blame on my mother. She did the best she could at that time.

Since I was overweight, I had a very difficult time keeping up with other children my age. Like I mentioned before, my family scoffed at my physical limitations as a side effect of being heavier than the other children. I always knew it was more than that. The older I became, the worse I felt. My classmates were always involved in sports and they loved physical education. This was truly beyond me. The last time I remember running, and actually liking it, was in kindergarten. "Why would any kid enjoy playing any sport?" I wondered.

I used to actually study the other kids while they ran around and played. I would ask myself, "How are they doing that?" Somehow they had some secret that I was not privy to. My legs were stiff and heavy and could not bend like the other kids that were running relays and skipping during recess.

My first real experience with consistent pain was when I was five years old. I started getting this intense pain in my eye. I would hold the top of my head and just cry. My mom would lay me down. I felt better in a dark room; I couldn't stand the light. "What is it mommy? Am I going to die?"

"No", my mom would assure me. She used to make a cup of tea and then come upstairs with the hot tea bag to put it on my eye. Although it did not do much for the pain, in my head and eye, it was calming and I liked it. I could not verbalize what I was feeling except that it was very intense and I always needed to go to bed. Sometimes I would get sick to my stomach. In preparation, my mom always kept coke-a-cola syrup in the house. Little did I realize, that this pain was the beginning of a life-long battle with migraine headaches.

I was eleven years old when my mother decided to take me on a trip to Europe, for a month, and then go stay with her family in South Africa for six months. It was a glorious trip. I had a really hard time keeping up with my mother who always had a fast gait. She seemed to be the human version of the Road Runner. We went to England, Ireland, Germany, France, Switzerland, Austria, and Italy. I can still picture the London Bridge, the Louvre, and Michelangelo's Sistine Chapel. I remember riding on a train through the Alps, and standing in a town square in Switzerland; we watched the life-size, coo-coo clock figures perform on the hour. It was a wonderful trip carefully planned by my mother who took me out of the sixth grade, much to the chagrin of my teacher, Mrs. Wilson.

We ended up in Cape Town where we stayed with our family. I decided (at the tender age of eleven) that I would stay in South Africa and never return to the States. I loved being with my enormous family. I had so many cousins and other relatives, and they embraced me into their world. To them, it didn't matter that I was big and awkward.

They pierced my ears with only a needle and thread, taught me how to "swirl" my hair with bobby pins to make it straight, and taught me "p" language. I still use "p" language with my best friend, Milly, when we are trying to keep a conversation private. I also brought home the card game called, "Spit", that my cousins and their children still play. The memories were epic. We took the cable car up to the top of Table Mountain, in Cape Town, and it was wondrous. I looked around from the top of the mountain and I knew that this is where I was belonged. This is where my mother belonged. This was our home.

When we returned, my depression began. I had gained 80 pounds during the six months we were gone–EIGHTY! I went from a world of low self-esteem, to a place where I received the most love I have ever known in my short life. But, perhaps, those six months were only a tableau. In the States, we returned back to the screaming, fighting, and insanity. The acute sense of loneliness was all encompassing.

As I grew older, I somehow became, in my mother's eyes, more unmanageable. She could be very reactive and before I knew it…. BAM! She'd hit me over the head with a heavy, glass ashtray or with a plate out of the kitchen cabinet. One time, she didn't like the expression on my face while I was talking on the phone, so she pulled the receiver out of my hand and banged me over the head with it multiple times.

My mom would toss whatever was nearest to her, full force, in my direction. I remember many a shoe grazing my head—sometimes I would get the belt, or be chased with a paddle—We would have knockdown, drag-out brawls. I was often confused about how, or why, these episodes even started. It tore me up inside. I could not be at peace until my mom and I talked and straightened things out by at least apologizing. I felt like the most despicable person on the face of the earth. None of my friends had physical fights with *their* mothers. I would wonder what I ever did to deserve this cycle of insanity. But there I was, ranting and raving along with my two parents. It's interesting how that happens.

My teenage years were rough ones. My father retired from the Merchant Marines when I was sixteen year old. I remember my mother sitting me down at the kitchen table to break the news. The look on her face communicated that something was very wrong. Her eyes welled with tears, and she said, "I'm sorry to have to tell you this but your father is retiring." "No!" I screamed. Her head nodded,

'yes', slowly. We sat in silence for what seemed like the longest time, crying. We both understood that life was about to change. We both wondered how we were going to survive it. My mother felt it more than me. She grieved. I just escaped.

At first, life in the little split-level 'Charm' home, on Maple Avenue in Lindenwold, appeared fine. I remember running upstairs with the utmost joy to tell my mother that I actually had a conversation with my father. That meant so much to me at the time. In the past, he talked and I just listened. Otherwise, he just sat and watched TV, and showed up at the dinner table at 5:30 pm sharp, and drank of course. At the time, I remember feeling badly for both of my parents. My father was demeaned and verbally abused by my mother. My mother was abandoned, cheated on, and at times, physically abused by my father. The clue that all hell was going to break loose, was when my father took off his glasses. The screaming was endless.

As an only child, I would often internalize that negative energy as my own. I thought I was the cause of it, somehow, or I was a bad kid because I couldn't stop it. When I got older, running away from the madness was my therapy of choice. I would retreat to the company of my friends. I have to say, that despite the chaos at home, I had a ball with my friends. We would party in the woods almost every night. On the weekends, we would go to the local sand pit and drink as much beer as we could tolerate. We often drove to the Pine Barrens, made bon fires, and laughed our butts off. We went to the shore, took our clothes off, and ran into the ocean. I had a very funny and imaginative group of friends at the time. We went everywhere and did everything. It was glorious. The same group of us stayed together for many years and grew together. Those days are among my most cherished memories.

I was a fearless teenager. I drank quite a bit, and I was called "a garbage head." I basically ingested whatever drug was available at the moment. I had no actual preference. I smoked cigarettes and pot regularly. During my senior year of high school, I collapsed in the cafeteria; the handful of Valium I was about to take went flying in every direction. I was so high that I just fell to the floor.

I struggled in school, both educationally and socially. I couldn't stand being in my own skin. I always felt awkward and never felt as thought I fit in anywhere. There was a bizarre kind of yin and yang happening in my soul. Love and hate went hand and hand. There were intensely good times and outrageously bad times. To date, this same pattern is evident in all my closest relationships: intense joy and laughter shared with many, and horrid sadness seen by a select few.

My isolation started to affect my behavior the first year of high school. I quickly realized that I was not going to be able to hide this secret of my physical pain and awkwardness during the hellish gym hour. "One of these things is not like the others," I would say to myself and laugh. I remember becoming nauseous and having visceral, internal, reactions that I did not understand. They started right before gym class. As a result, I decided that avoiding gym was the answer.

I remember using the "I left my gym clothes at home" excuse. That didn't last long. I think gym teachers can sniff out the kids who have anxiety with the class, and, as a result, love to make us sweat. I decided not showing up for class was the answer.

However, cutting class only backfired. I failed the class. In order to graduate, I had to take gym in my senior year, twice. I changed schools during my sophomore year due to the amount of trouble I was in for that. I used the same tactic at the new school. That's why it didn't all catch up to me until my senior year.

The interesting thing was that during those few years I had lost a significant amount of weight, around sixty pounds. I was so used to my mother blame everything on weight, so I was baffled when my aches and pains continued even after the weight loss. "I can't even lose weight right", I thought. "I look better, but I don't feel better." What is up with this?

I remember once spending the day at the mall with my friends. I remember I had a dull ache in my legs and feet, which only grew by the hour. As the day went on, I moved more slowly, and could not seem to keep up with my friends. It was beyond me how they could keep going. Aren't they tired? Aren't they sore too? I still had the "fat and lazy" tapes running through my head from elementary school. I wondered: Did everybody feel the same way, but just not talk about it?

This was a common theme during my young, adult life as I went on trips to the beach, or attended school dances, or just experienced physical activity. But I got used to it. It never stopped me. I ran with the pack and danced until the sun came up. Life was good. I knew I was not destined to compete in the Olympics, but that was fine with me. I had nothing in common with jocks anyway.

CHAPTER 4

The Flickering Light

When I was a child attending a Catholic school, God was unapproachable spirit who was busy in heaven running things. He knew all things (like Santa Claus), especially if I was bad and sinned. If I sinned, it would infuriate God, and, as a result, he might send me to a place called Purgatory after I died. Although it was better than Hell, which was the next step, it was still a terrible place to linger. If I were, in fact, bad, I would be cast into limbo with only the anticipation of Hell. I would be stuck there with the pagan babies that died before they were baptized. Furthermore, thunder and lightening existed, because God got really mad. Ergo, it was up to the nuns to turn us into good Catholic girls and boys.

I was always fascinated with God. I wondered about Him. Although we had such fear instilled in us, I knew God was a loving Father. That is what my mother taught me. The problem: I didn't know what it meant to have a loving father. A very dead Jesus hung on a huge cross in front of our church. Dead Jesus always made me very sad; I felt as though I had somehow killed Him. I was taught that my actions could make Dead Jesus cry. My ill behavior made God hang His head with disappointment. God cried when I got annoyed with my classmate. Therefore, I should be punished.

Apparently, the only way to survive this evil within me was to go to a priest for absolution. I had to tell the priest about all of the things I did wrong, and then recite the prayers he recommended. Then I could attend Mass and rest assured that I would not be going to Hell. (That week anyway). It helped if I said the rosary; call it an insurance of sorts. I paid special attention in religion class and earned good grades. It was important to know about God and Dead Jesus. My mom and I would pray every night on our knees. We asked God to forgive us for our sins and to bless our family. One wouldn't want to accidentally die and be pulled down to Hell, with the devil, for not doing homework.

I was seventeen years old when I realized that God, through his grace, sent Jesus to die in my stead. Although I asked the Lord to come into my life, I did not develop a relationship with God. Instead, I continued to smoke, drink, and take drugs, which only killed my witness and made me feel badly about myself. That was something I was quite used to. I let sin control me.

My mother's sister, Poppy, and her husband, Dick, used to take me to their church, which I really enjoyed. These services were starkly different than the masses I went to at the Catholic Church. There was serious preaching and worshipping, and I didn't totally understand what was happening, but I knew that I liked it. This greatly upset my parents. They were concerned that I was writing-off Catholicism and becoming a "Jesus freak." Just what I needed in my life, more turmoil and conflict!

The good news: I have always had an open mind. The bad news: I have always had an open mind. Over the course of my life, this has been both to my benefit, and also to my detriment. I never cared what other people thought, one way or another. I never considered popular opinion, whether it was good, bad, or indifferent. I lived one situation at a time.

The summer of my fifteenth year, my aunt, uncle, four cousins, and I headed up to Pine Crest Bible School in Upstate New York for the weekend. It was a combination of dorm-like rooms with a cabin-type feel. Bunk beds and spiders are all I can remember about the accommodations—NOT a happy combination for me!—the other children attending this retreat, ran around playing games I didn't know, and sang songs I'd never heard. It was awkward. I wondered how long it would take me to get home if I left there in the middle of the night.

But, the grounds there at Pine Crest were beautiful. It was nestled far back in the most stunning wooded area I had ever seen. One day, I remember feeling uncomfortable, yet again, in the crowd; I decided to take a long walk into the woods, alone. I traversed many trails and followed the beams of light that danced brightly through the trees. I saw the clouds billow, and change, and felt the warm breeze tickle my skin. I felt elated. It was then that I started to talk to God. I mean, really talk. I asked Him why things had to happen the way they did, and what was the point of everything. I walked along the moss-filled path, and I knew I wasn't alone. I knew Jesus was there, walking with me.

All of a sudden, I started to cry. It wasn't a whimper or moan. This was a guttural lament that came from a place of deep pain and despair. I released it—all my pain. I presented it to God. I realized that my life had a plan and a purpose. God knew all of it. He had his hand on me and He wasn't letting go. It was that day, in the woods at Pine Crest Bible School, that I was touched by God (metaphorically speaking).

There was a Christian organization in the town of Vineland, New Jersey called, Mission Teens, which was about a forty-minute drive from my home. Parents sent their troubled teens and runaways there, although, some enrolled voluntarily. Others, however, were court ordered. It was an old, run-down building full of cockroaches. On Wednesday nights, a group of us would drive down and meet the residents in the main parlor to gather for Bible study and prayer meetings. We would bring a dozen donuts as a snack. I always noticed the residents staring wide-eyed at the donut box. I thought we might need a mop to wipe the drool off their chins. That was always sad to me.

Additionally, Mission Teens sponsored retreats. They charged a minimal fee, and we would have weekend-long versions of those Wednesday night services. During those retreats, I learned that the Mission Teens' building had rats in addition to the roaches. We would sleep in bunk beds, and pull the covers tightly over our heads for fear of a critter taking up residency in some orifice of our body. I would lie awake wondering why I was there. Never again, I would say…until the next retreat.

The draw for me was in the worship at Mission Teens. The Holy Spirit was shaking the place on a regular basis. There was no denying it. God was moving in a mighty way there. It was on one of those retreat weekends that I was baptized in the Spirit! I was eighteen years old, and it was an experience I will never forget! I knew the Lord had changed me that day and I would never be the same again!

But it was also a difficult time for me. I had no spiritual guidance, and life at home was explosive. I had no church home, nor any Christian people that I could be vulnerable with in general. I couldn't talk to my family. So, I felt like I never had the opportunity to grow and mature as a Christian.

As a result, during my young adult years I played the backsliding game. One month I was toting my Bible to prayer meetings, and the next month I was copping an ounce of pot on the corner. God spared my life. He was gracious to me, during these years; there were many times I made bad choices and did very stupid things. Despite all the chemicals I ingested during this time, I still felt pain. My legs and feet started to swell and become uncomfortable. The stiffness and extreme fatigue followed me through my mid-twenties.

CHAPTER 5

The Machine

When pain takes up residency in our bodies, it is the beginning of a long journey. Many of us do not acknowledge it exists until we have no choice. Pain triggers the fight-or-flight response in our bodies—this puts us in an almost constant state of stress—and it wears us down. When we finally go to the doctor, we receive either unclear answers or no answers at all. If we do get an answer, we're told that there are one hundred different ways to treat it. Each particular physician has his or her own philosophy of treatment. They are medicine men, physical therapy supporters, and those who are surgery happy. Some doctors even use a more holistic approach.

However, before treatment, we have to go for testing. We have to endure long, painful procedures that often produce no results. We are x-rayed, scanned, poked, prodded, and pinched. One doctor might send us to a multitude of other doctors that might repeat the same testing process. This can go on for years.

Searching for a proper diagnosis creates so much frustration on the part of the patient. When a doctor cannot make a diagnosis, and assumes the problem is "psychogenic" or even worse, "psychosomatic" in nature, it leaves a heavy burden on the patient. In other words, they think we are nuts! Suddenly, we assume the role of doctor in order to search, and study, different diagnosis ourselves. It is our responsibility to take care of our health, but are we supposed to be the healers too? Medicine is not an exact science. What will help one person might not help another. Each person must consider all the options, and try various remedies, until he or she finds something that works: Diet, Exercise, Medications, Supplements, Surgery, Acupuncture, Biofeedback, Chinese Medicine, Chiropractic Medicine, Electromagnetic Therapy, Homeopathic Remedies, Hypnosis, Ice/Warm Compresses, Massage and Pain Management. All these options exist just to treat a burning, dull ache, or a sharp piercing pain brought on by a chronic disease.

Consequently, we read articles, and medical journals, to determine the latest and best practices on treatment for our respective chronic illnesses. We might even have multiple issues akin to Fibromyalgia, a herniated disc, and Lymphedema.

One early, May evening, I sat at my kitchen table and studied for my exams. It was a stressful time since all of my final projects were due. I started to feel something akin to indigestion; I assumed it was caused by the stress I felt building in my body. I took my dog for a walk in an effort to maneuver the gas, and bloating, out of my stomach. This did not work. The discomfort in my stomach got worse, so I went to bed. In the middle of the night, I called for my mother. She then woke up my father, and the three of us trekked to the local emergency room. I do not remember the initial diagnosis, but I remember that they gave me some pain medication and told me to go home. After being home only a few hours, I became violently ill. Namely, I had a fever and I could not stop vomiting.

First thing in the morning, my parents took me directly to our family doctor. He said that we had to go back to the emergency room since he suspected I had appendicitis. This time I was kept in the hospital because I was so ill. I was admitted into the hospital in the early hours of the next day. The hospital took their time doing tests. That Monday, I was in the bathroom when I felt a pain like I had never felt before. It was like an explosion in my gut. I thought I was going to pass out. I pulled the cord and the nurse came running. She asked me what was wrong, and I told her that I had a severe pain in my stomach. She told me is was probably gas and walked away. I remember thinking that I have had gas before and it never felt like this. I was doubled over and barely made it to my hospital bed.

After that, I started to go down-hill quickly. My insides felt like they were eroding. The doctor ordered many test. I remember the doctor pacing back and forth in my room. He kept muttering that my white blood cell count was high, and he didn't know the cause. The preliminary diagnosis was inflammatory pelvic disease. I asked how a person gets that, and they responded, "dirty sex." I looked at doctor and reminded him that I was a virgin. The doctor, and nurses, just looked at me and walked out of the room. I was emotionally devastated, but too sick to react. I started drifting more and more into a complete physical shutdown. I didn't speak or eat. All I did was sleep. I was hooked up to a host of machines.

It was during this time, that a friend came to visit me. I would whisper, "come closer", and just hold her hand. I was too sick to communicate how terrified I was. All I wanted to do was sleep. In fact, my strength was draining out of me with each passing hour. I felt like I was just slipping away.

The doctor decided to perform exploratory surgery. As they wheeled me into the operating room, I remember praying, "Your will be done not mine, Lord." The surgeon and medical team were amazed at what they found when they opened me. My appendix had ruptured. I had peritonitis. The doctor found tiny pieces of what was left of my appendix. I had an incision from my belly button all the way down to the lowest part of my stomach, as well as three, huge, sideways cuts. My surgeon divulged that he poured saline solution into my stomach because my organs were inflamed. I had a massive infection due to the peritonitis. The biggest tragedy was that the peritonitis had eroded my reproductive organs and fallopian tubes. I was told that I had only a twenty percent chance of ever having children.

I remember hearing the nurse talking to me in the recovery room. She kept repeating, "Maureen, wake up." I wanted so bad to respond. "Come on, Maureen, open your eyes." There was a tube down my throat and it was making me gag. I couldn't open my eyes; I couldn't move. I just wanted this tube out of my throat, but I couldn't tell them that I was awake. It felt like hours before a nurse noticed that I was moving my hand. She asked me if I understood her. I signaled that I did. I felt like I was in some house of horrors. Eventually, the tube was removed. Afterwards, I was on many strong antibiotics to fight the infection.

The doctor brought many rounds of his medical residents into my room, and talked about me as if I wasn't there. He introduced me as, "the one who lived", *Ahhhh*, they all gasped, as if they had heard about, "Maureen the Legend" who resides here in this bed. Some of them looked at me intently, and others smiled at me as if to say, "Congratulations, you made it!"

The students asked my surgeon questions about what happened. But, I could not understand a word. It was just too much medical mumbo-jumbo; plus, I was so weak I could barley stay awake. Soon, the nurses started pouring in just to get a look. They also kept referring to me as, "The one who lived."

Several nurses from the operating room came to see me. They held my hand, and told me how happy they were to see me since I had been very close to death. The one I really wanted to see, was that nurse who told me (probably at the moment my appendix ruptured), that I simply had gas. I also wanted to clear myself of the "inflammatory pelvic disease" stigma as well. I was very negatively affected by that accusation.

I remained in that hospital for one month. I left there a much thinner, weaker, but more grateful, me. I grieved, up until the age of forty, that I was not able to bear children as a result of the ruptured appendix. Later, I came to believe that it was a small price to pay for my life.

CHAPTER 6

The Old College Try

Character cannot be developed in ease and quiet. Only through experience and trial and suffering can the soul be strengthened, vision cleared, ambition inspired, and success achieved. —Helen Keller

I was married in the church I attended growing up, St. Lawrence, in June of 1986. My husband was seven years younger than me. We had a big, lavish wedding with all the trimmings. We never saw our second wedding anniversary.

We had just found a house to move into when we separated. Luckily, I did buy that house, but it was in my name only. My father took the separation worse than my mother, which surprised me. He just kept asking me what I was going to do. I assured him that I would be fine. Naturally, I lied.

I cried non-stop after I moved into my house. For six weeks, I cried every waking moment. I literally, woke up crying and went to sleep crying. I remember shopping at the grocery store and not caring that I would cry my head off, while the other shoppers looked at me with comforting eyes. I even cried at work. It was amazing. I stopped crying as suddenly as I started, six weeks later. Luckily, I had my career to distract me from my failed marriage.

I graduated from college with an Associate of Science Degree in Interpreting for the Deaf from Union County College. They offered a satellite program at Camden County College in Blackwood, New Jersey. I did well at Camden County College; I ascertained a surprisingly high grade point average. I loved my field of choice since I'd been friends with many deaf, and hard of hearing, people since I was sixteen. One week after my college graduation, my mother walked into my room, pulled the covers off of me, and said, "It's time to go get a job." I remember shuddering after I pulled the covers back. But, mom was right. I had to go and establish myself. It was time to start my career.

I did not have a dependable car, so I often used public transportation to travel to my interpreting assignments. I vividly remember running for the train, or down a city block, to make it to my job on time. Waiting for buses or trains, often made the sharp pain in my feet more intense. I thought to myself, so this is how crippled people feel. What a strange thought for such a young person. I was in the "nothing is going to stop me" mode then. It was difficult, but it was possible.

Interpreting jobs could often last many hours without a break. One particular day, I was working a four hour assignment alone. There was a big group of Deaf people, and the only way to interpret visibly was to stand. Naturally, this was one of those assignments where the hearing people in the group voted to see if they wanted a break. Nah, they decided to keep going, and forget about the sign language interpreter! When the assignment was over, I was instructed where to go to get my check. I went to the accounting department where they informed me that I had to walk to the next building—the length of a city block—in order to collect my money. When the woman told me that, I looked at her and burst out crying.

I hobbled out of the building and wondered how I would make it to the next building. There was no way I could do it. My feet were so swollen that I could barely fit them into my shoes. The pain was overwhelming. I finally admitted that I had a problem; it was time to find out what was going on.

"I'm in pain!" I let myself think, finally. That was a serious AH HA, moment. That was the beginning. The next day I made an appointment with my doctor.

My doctor stared at me for what seemed like a very long time. I had just told her what happened when trying to collect my check. I could tell that she considered my words carefully, and that she was working through something in her mind. She conducted an initial exam, and decided that she wanted to get a full battery of x-rays. A few days after I had completed the series of x-rays, my doctor called me at home. She told me to make another appointment with her.

My doctor entered the office while staring at my chart. She did not make eye contact with me, which I thought seemed strange. "I wanted to talk to you in person, Maureen. I am disturbed by the results of your x-rays and want to talk about a treatment plan. You have significant osteoarthritis in your feet and your knees. However, the worst is in your hips. I predict that you have, perhaps, five years left on your right hip before it will need to be replaced."

It was now my turn to stare at the doctor for a long time. All of the sudden, I started to laugh. "This is insane! You've got the x-rays mixed up with some old lady," I interjected. She looked into my eyes and said, very seriously, "No, I'm sorry, but these are your x-rays". I left the office thinking, "Well, ok, I have five years before I have to worry about that."

֎

Chronic illness can play havoc with your bank account for a variety of reasons. Namely, pain is the leading cause of lost workdays. Financial hardship ensues if a person does not have sick days, as part of a benefit package, through their place of employment. Those of us who do have sick days available, often have chronic absences and use them up quickly. This can lead to termination for many of us. We are left with no income, no medical insurance, and no prescription coverage, which is a recipe for disaster. We are then offered COBRA coverage through the state for a limited time. This coverage can cost up to $700.00 per month, for an individual plan, and over $1,000 for a family plan. This is like paying a mortgage.

Few people have the financial freedom to continue their coverage when they are chronically ill. Therefore, we push ourselves to continue working as long as we possibly can. Another cost to consider is the deductible, which can often be quite steep—add on the frequent trips to various doctors, and perhaps physical therapy or other expensive treatments—these are just a few of the reasons that a bank account can be quickly depleted.

There are countless other expenses to consider when you suffer from an ongoing condition. We must also pay for our braces, special wraps, traction devices, wheelchairs, shower seats, raised toilet seats, walkers, lift chairs, grab bars, orthopedic shoes, car adaptations, hospital beds, bedside tables, scooters, etc.. The list goes on infinitely. Some of these can be considered a luxury item, but most are essential for everyday living.

There is generally a long wait after applying for Social Security Disability, that is, if your doctor agrees that your condition warrants it. It can take years, and some folks must hire an attorney after being denied multiple times. Sometimes you could wait two years after being approved in order to be eligible for Medicare benefits. This is why we are often wrought with worry regarding our financial circumstances, and what the future holds, in addition to being ill. It results in a prolonged state of stress for many families.

However, the Bible says that God is faithful. We should cast our cares upon the Lord. He knows what we are going through, and He knows our needs.

CHAPTER 7

The Buddy

Buck Hazelton was husband number two. Dear old, dysfunctional Buck. We first met, one ordinary evening, when I was interpreting at a Narcotics Anonymous meeting. A huge guy, full of tattoos, approached me to ask if I knew who was teaching the summer course, in Basic American Sign Language, at Camden County College. I looked up at him and said, "I am."

He proceeded to explain how he wanted to help deaf addicts. *Here we go again,* I thought to myself. I had met my first husband in AA. Buck's 6'4" frame hovered over me. He was still talking but I wasn't listening. All I could think of was how much I loved the sound of his deep voice. *Stop it, Maureen. We are not going there again.*

The Basic American Sign-Language class commenced during the summer of 1988. It was wonderful. Eventually, I learned that Buck was married. However, being Eunice's daughter, this was an unacceptable attraction. I determined that I would deny myself, totally and completely, which is what I did.

One day, I was running a little late. When I arrived to the classroom, everybody was waiting for me out in the hallway. The shoulder pad in my dress was twisted when I initially approached Buck. He noticed the pad, stuck his hand in my dress, and fixed it. The class noticed the awkward familiarity; you could hear a pin drop. I remember looking at the class and saying, "We know each other." That of course, was a lie.

Buck and I would often stay after class to talk and laugh. There was a loud voice telling me that this was not right! I wish I listened.

I knew he had a wife and a son.

After our friendship developed, I decided I needed a dose of reality, so I invited Buck's family over. I thought that it was important for me to get to know Buck's wife. She turned out to be a very nice woman. I felt that Buck should do whatever it took to save his marriage. At that time, his son was only four years old. And he was adorable.

I would not let Buck into my home if it was just the two of us hanging out. It wasn't him I didn't trust. It wasn't appropriate and that was that. However, I found myself constantly thinking about Buck and talked about him often. My friends knew that I was falling for him before I did.

I had met Buck in June of 1988. I noticed that my friendship with him was changing, but didn't understand just how much. At some point, I even stopped noticing what was really happening; I started living in a fantasy world. This went on until one day, when Buck and I were casually talking, something unexpected came out of my mouth. I said, without thinking, "I wish we could always be together." Buck looked at me and I remember standing there idiotically, wondering, "Where did *that* come from?"

Up to that point in our friendship, there had been NO physical contact between us because, contrary to popular belief, I really did want the best for him and his family.

The night that my father passed away, in September, Buck and his wife came to my house. I didn't understand the feelings that overcame me when I saw her with him. I felt uncomfortable, and almost angry. In retrospect, I felt jealous—but I knew I had no right to be jealous—so it just turned into anger instead. When Buck agreed to be a pallbearer, I felt like he was "mine" for the few minutes it would take to carry my father's body; and then, all was right in the world.

A few days later, Buck called. He said that he needed to come over and talk about something very important. I had no idea what to expect. I could see that he was very nervous when he walked through the door. "What is it, Buck?" I asked. "This is really hard for me," he said. "Out with it, it's just me," I said trying to reassure him. "That's the problem," he said. I took him by the hand, and looked into his eyes. I waited silently to hear this horrible earth shattering news.

"I'm in love with you," he said.

Oh my God, Oh my God…OH MY GOD! Say it isn't so! I felt like somebody had just shot me between the eyes. How did I let this happen? Did I do this? Did my feelings, the ones I did not even admit to myself, cause this? What have I done? I knew that physically there had not been a touch exchanged between us, but still. I also knew that I would be blamed, and labeled, as "the home-wrecker" for the rest of my life! That is exactly what happened.

Minutes after Buck told me that he was in love with me, I asked him to leave. I told him that I did not want to see him anymore, and that he should forget his feelings for me. I was very adamant about not seeing him again. Emotional affairs like this, start in the mind way before they develop into physical contact. I knew that. I begged him to go for marriage counseling and repair his marriage for the sake of his son. I asked him not to contact me.

A few days later, I was sitting, reading sympathy cards, at my dining room table when a knock came at my door. It was Buck's wife, and his mother, asking if I had seen him. I shook my head "no", and asked why. They told me that Buck had moved out. Not only had he moved out, but he left them on his son's fifth birthday. I was beside myself. I felt that I should be tarred and feathered. I didn't have the slightest clue where Buck went, but I did know that our involvement made it easier for him to leave his family.

The days and weeks that followed were ugly. There were many fights and arguments, on the street in front of my house, between his wife, Jess, and myself. I felt humiliated in front of my neighbors. The last time Jessica visited, she accused me of stealing her husband. I told her that it had always been my wish for them to reconcile, especially for Christian's sake. But, from that moment on, I would welcome a relationship with Buck. And I did.

Sometimes, I would dream that I was waiting for an elevator.

In the dream, the doors would finally open, and Jess and Christian would emerge motionless. They were always dressed in sackcloth and had dirt smudged on their faces. Those nightmares stayed with me for a long time.

Buck and I were married at the church we had been attending, Laurel Hill Bible Church, on August 10, 1990. Buck was the absolute love of my life. At that time, I saw my husband as a very kind man. He was a good caretaker for my mom and I. Buck had his problems, but he was such a good husband. He wasn't much of a provider, but he made up for it in other ways.

I depended a lot on Buck. He did the shopping and the cooking and the cleaning and the laundry. *Whew!* Domestic responsibilities were Buck's strength, and he did them well. We lived in a section of Camden, New Jersey called, Fairview, in a lovely, brick, corner row home. It was surrounded by a neighborhood rich in history.

Buck and I were very happy. We did all the things that lovers do. We took scenic walks, held hands, and strolled to the local ice cream parlor on summer nights. We read poetry by candlelight, and enjoyed the fragrance of the white impatiens, and ivy, growing in the flower boxes on the front porch. We loved sitting on the porch during storms—we loved the whir of thunder, the wonderment of lightning—and if we got soaked, we never minded. It was our world, and we were the only ones in it. This honeymoon feeling lasted for many years of our marriage.

We went all out at Christmas time. Mom bought Buck a beautiful Santa Claus costume for Christmas one year. After that, he often paraded around as Santa for friends. Later, I made a Mrs. Claus outfit, and we went out performing as a team. It was great fun. Buck would decorate the house, and he put a large speaker outside, on the porch, to play Christmas music. We often won awards for the best decorated house. Everybody flocked to our house over the holidays. We had so many traditions. Our favorite tradition: We played Michael Jackson videos and danced while decorating the Christmas tree. We would also meet our friends at church for the annual candlelight service.

We loved going to Lancaster, PA to drive around the Amish country. Buck and I took an interest in the simple life of the Amish people. We always wished we could be Amish. We took long drives on the back roads and farms of the Amish countryside. And we often got lost.

Buck and I had a wonderful life for many years. He was my lover, my best friend, and my caretaker. Buck often called me his "heart of hearts". We shared many of the same interests and had fun at almost every turn. We went to church together, read the Bible together, and prayed together. I was so much in love with him. We laughed together constantly, and cried together when the need arose. We had a really intense union. We could actually finish each other's sentences before we even spoke them. We were that connected. Simply put, I adored him. He understood me better than anybody else. I felt so lucky to have found such a wonderful mate.

However, there was a side of Buck that was very difficult to live with. If he got into his mind, that he didn't like something, or somebody, he was quite vocal about it. His large stature made him appear threatening. Once Buck got moody, that was it. We had verbal exchanges that were very similar to the ones I shared with my mother growing up. In fact, Buck and I maintained something akin to the love/hate relationship I had with my mother at times. I was quite skilled in this style of arguing, so Buck finally ceased his attempts to manipulate and control me. He learned that it was useless, and that screaming and bullying were futile.

The five years, that my primary physician predicted my hip would last, was drawing to a close. My gait had slowed tremendously. My hip would lock in the middle of walking. That was agony. Intimacy became quite difficult as well. I knew that I had to get a job with good medical benefits. I found a great position as a full-time Sign Language Interpreter at Camden County College. I had graduated their four years earlier. I was thrilled! This job offered me everything I needed to satisfy my health benefits and my career goals!

I received my handicapped driver's license plates in the mail on my 30th birthday. How bizarre is that? I was floored by it. *I mean, on my birthday?* C'mon. It was around that time, when my husband suggested I use a cane. I was opposed at first, and told him to take a hike. He was a patient man. We went for a ride to Lancaster, Pennsylvania and found this really neat cane made out of the strongest, maple wood. It was the perfect height for me and it fit my personality.

My husband had won the cane argument. I started using the cane. I was pleasantly surprised how much it did help me. It did not stop the hip from locking, but it helped me put less pressure on that hip. My colleagues and I named my cane, "The Buddy". I tried to be light hearted about my health. I couldn't hide it anymore because I would scream if the hip locked while walking around in the office. I am not a silent sufferer for the most part. If I said I needed, "The Buddy," a coworker would walk to my office and get my cane for me. I made the people around me part of my treatment plan, and they did not seem to mind.

When I went to see a surgeon, he thought that I could wait one more year. He said that he did not like to operate on young people. He was also not pleased with my weight, which ballooned up after I got married. My husband was a cook in the navy. He cooked and baked and loved to serve up a full plate. Due to my lack of mobility, and my slow metabolism, everything I put into my mouth seemed to turned to fat. Of course, I was delighted with the doctor's decision, but suddenly wondered how I was going to get through the next year. "How will I make it to all those buildings with just a ten minute break in between? There are so many people rushing around, almost knocking me over, especially to get on the elevator". Somehow, I did it.

A year later, I returned to the surgeon to schedule the hip replacement surgery. I had to go to classes before the surgery. During a class, I mentioned that I had a lot of widespread pain, and asked if it was from leaning on the cane. Once again, I just assumed that everybody was as sore all over, and fatigued, as I was. After all, when one of your joints is not working properly, it affects the entire body, right? Apparently not.

The nurse suggested that I go to my doctor to get checked for Fibromyalgia. I went to my rheumatologist to follow up on the nurse's suggestion. Lo and behold, after my exam, my doctor said, "Yep, you have all the classic symptoms of Fibromyalgia". I was shocked. I did not realize how up-to-date my rheumatologist's office was, until that time. At that time, nobody knew much about Fibromyalgia. Most doctors didn't believe in it. This was a debate among physicians that continued for years. There were pain pressure points, and other symptoms such as irritable bowel syndrome, and migraine headaches. I had all of the symptoms on the list. Because we had been regularly attending Laurel Hill Bible Church, I had, by this time, received enough spiritual nurturing to know that the Lord had blessed me up until that point. I was confident that He wasn't going to let go of me now.

CHAPTER 8

Hip Hip Hooray

When my surgery was finally approved, a date was set for August 12, 1991. I was thirty-one years old. I woke up in the recovery room and felt okay. When I got to my room, my husband, my mother, and my friends were there staring at me with concern and compassion. Later, when I woke up, I was glad my husband was still there. As the evening went on, I started feeling more and more pain. I was connected to a morphine pump. But, no matter how many times I pushed the button, nothing was happening. The pain kept getting more and more intense. I was starting to hit the morphine machine continuously with my arm. I needed relief.

The nurse came in the room, assured me that there was nothing wrong and, said that I had to just endure it. They allowed my husband to stay in the room with me during the night. He was there, gently caressing me, and comforting me, and taking care of me. He knew something was drastically wrong. At one point, he went out to the nurse's station and started yelling that there was something wrong with his wife. "My wife can take a lot of pain. Something is wrong and you are going to fix it now!" They had just finished a shift change making it about 7:00 am in the morning. A nurse came immediately. She checked my intravenous line and discovered that it was not in my vein! The nurse also noticed that my arm was very swollen. This indicated that all the fluid was being absorbed into the surrounding tissue. The woman was mortified. We all deduced that I had received NO pain medicine at all after my surgery. This was brutal.

I remember the way my husband looked at me—tears filled up in his eyes—he whispered, "Baby, I just can't imagine what you just went through. If I knew, I would have had it fixed earlier." This is when the doctor decided to put a central line into the artery in my neck. My doctor came in the room, gave me some local anesthesia, and cut a small hole in my neck that lead to an artery. Before I knew it, I had mega amounts of pain medicine flowing and I immediately fell asleep. Unfortunately, I had massive bruises on my arm where I had been hitting the morphine pump all night.

The first week after my surgery, I stayed at my mother's house. I didn't want to do anything. I couldn't sleep, I didn't want to eat, and I had no interest in television or reading. I felt so uncomfortable. I had fifty-five staples in my hip; they stretched from top of my hip, down to my buttocks. It was red and swollen, and it looked like a bayonet wound from the Civil War. I kept complaining that it felt like someone sewed a machine gun in my hip. All my colleagues would come by on their lunch hour and visit because my mother lived so close to the college. My leg looked so gross to them. All of the staples and severe swelling made many of them gasp. Some of my colleagues told me they didn't want to eat their lunches after visiting! It wasn't a pretty sight.

CHAPTER 9

R-E-S-P-E-C-T

I began experiencing a strange feeling in my toes. I told my mom that my toes felt funny. My mom would rub my feet and it felt better. Soon after, I experienced a feeling akin to pins and needle in my foot. I contacted the doctor. He thought it was my body's way of adjusting to the new hip, especially since I was lying around a lot more than I was used to. I accepted this explanation for about one day.

Next, came a feeling of burning and electricity. It was as though invisible parts of the sun broke off and landed on my foot. This burning sensation, this feeling of electrocution was excruciating. Finally, I had to leave my mother's house and go home. I could not believe the amount of pain, and the strange type of numbness, I had in my foot. I finally went to the doctor; he told me it could be gout. He suggested that I drink cherry juice.

During that time, pure cherry juice was hard to find. My husband went from store to store searching, and finally found a quart of cherry juice. He rushed home and poured me a glass of juice hoping that soon this new pain would lessen. It didn't. Not only did the cherry juice not bring relief, but the situation also became worse. My leg jumped in the air involuntarily. It could not handle anything that touched it. Even the soft breeze of a September afternoon caused a sharp, hot feeling of being electrocuted.

My husband tried to make light of the situation. Namely, he made jokes about the things I did when I stood up. I would often twist my leg a certain way, in order to stand on my foot. We called this, "The Elvis", which was pretty funny, because it did look like one of Elvis's popular dance moves. My legs twisted one way, and then twisted another. I did "The Elvis" every time I stood up.

The night hours were horrible; I could never sleep. I cried constantly. I could barely stand a sheet resting on my foot. My husband maintained a day job and received very little sleep, because he catered to my needs: he tried to comfort me all hours of the night. As a result, I manufactured guilt. I could neither control the pain, nor control how I was reacting to it. My best friend called me every day; I felt bad crying to her as well. But she just kept calling.

Our assistant church pastor could see the extent of my suffering, and would call or visit often. Suddenly, everything became about my foot, and not my recent hip replacement. My surgeon was satisfied with my recovery, although I still had to go to physical therapy. I have always hated physical therapy. It wasn't the actual therapy that I hated, but the person telling me what to do all the time. I guess my distain was focused on the physical therapist. I used to call them physical terrorists. However, the therapy did help me increase my ability to manage my new hip.

By this time, I had become very depressed. I felt that an unseen monster was controlling my life. Someone suggested that I go to a neurologist at this time. To them, my foot problems sounded like classic nerve pain. I made an appointment with a local neurologist; he was from India. I did not want to like him for some reason, but I did.

I was certain that the test he was about to conduct would kill me. I was wrong. He interviewed me for a long time, and administered a few tests that were not bad. He looked at me and said, you have Reflex Sympathetic Dystrophy. RSD, he said. "What?" I thought, "r-e-s-p-e-c-t, what is this man talking about?" He told me that many people in India had this problem, mostly in their wrist. Apparently, RSD is the feeling of pain associated with the evidence of minor nerve injury. The neurologist was convinced it was from the hip replacement. The prognosis was not good: very rarely did RSD go away. In fact, at times, it spreads. I thought, "Just give me the gun now, because if I have to live with this forever, I'll kill myself. I'll end up in a straight jacket. I won't be able to take this everyday for the rest of my life".

The doctor told me that he was sorry to give me that news. He also gave me an anti-seizure medicine, Dilantin, to help with the nerve pain. Immediately, after starting the medication, I felt so bizarre. I could not continue taking Dilantin for more than a few days. It made me feel like I was in one of Timothy Leary's LSD focus groups.

I went to visit my rheumatologist that originally diagnosed the Fibromyalgia. I thought for sure he would know how to help me, quickly and easily. There was discussion about putting a nerve block with screws inside of my ankle. When I left there, I cried hysterically. "No way", I thought. "No screws in my ankle, or anywhere else for that matter". My rheumatologist mentioned physical therapy as well. "I can do that", I thought. I went back to the same office that treated me for my hip. They knew me: the good, the bad and the ugly. They were aware of my limitations and capabilities. My husband was always beside me—he encouraged me, he pushed me, and he consoled me—it made me feel good, but also guilty. I felt that my ailments had disrupted our lives, and that it was an enormous burden for Buck.

However, this therapy was not bad at all. I did a few exercises with my ankle; I could tolerate that with no problem. Next, we did a warm whirlpool for my calf. I was surprised that my foot could tolerate it. In the beginning, therapy was rough. But, as the weeks went on, it all got much easier. I noticed that the frequency of lightning-type pain had diminished, and my leg stopped jumping in the air. Slowly, the pain in my foot decreased. There was no more doing, "The Elvis" when I stood up. I started using my sheets again. It was working! The physical therapy was working! In spite of the very small odds for success, the physical therapy worked. I recently learned that RSD rarely goes into remission. While physical therapy is used to decrease the intensity of RSD, it usually does not cause the condition to cease.

CHAPTER 10

Juggling

It doesn't matter how slowly you go
so long as you do not stop. —Confucius

For a number of years, I dealt well with the fibromyalgia, and back spasms, which alone was a challenge. I walked with a cane for a time, but eventually that went away too. I was doing great. At least in comparison to my recovery from the hip replacement and RSD, I was doing great. I glided along without many kinks in the road. I continued on with my personal life and career. I traveled for my job and gave lectures in different parts of the country. My coworkers would handle my luggage for me, if we all went on a business trip. I was also running across campus from building to building and, on occasion, climbing stairs when necessary.

It was difficult, but I created a system that worked for me. I knew what time to leave my office to beat the mad rush of students entering or exiting a building. I became familiar with the best door to enter and researched what corridor was the easiest route to my class.

My colleagues helped more than they even realized. When the walk from the car to the office was too much for me, I would call my office and ask someone to come meet me at my car. Later, I started driving around campus instead of walking. My colleagues did my errands for me. They delivered my important correspondences to different buildings on campus. They went to the copy center and picked up, or dropped off, things that needed to be copied. They moved office furniture. If I had a rough day, a staff member would run ahead and start my class. This allowed me to arrive at my own pace. I never felt so grateful to work with that wonderful group of people. After many years of working together, my coworkers seemed like family.

At home, my husband continued to take care of the majority of domestic responsibilities. I had very little energy left in me after arriving home from work. I always felt such immense guilt for dumping all of the shopping, cleaning, and laundry on Buck. He was very quick and thorough when executing a task. He always said he didn't mind, but I knew it was hard on him. I felt like the "loser wife" and that feeling was very hard to shake.

❦

I still have very little patience when it comes to depending on others. In fact, it makes me irritable. For instance, many people do not understand what happens if they cancel an appointment with me. Today, the woman who cleans my house for me, Lois, was supposed to come at 4 pm. In anticipation of her arrival, I woke up early to take care of some things. I also planned on asking her to stop at the store for me, as she often does, before she arrives, or once she has finished cleaning. Today, I needed something from the store that could not wait until tomorrow. Unfortunately, Lois called me at 3:50 pm to cancel. We rescheduled for tomorrow, but had I known, I would have spent my day differently. And perhaps I would have spent my day differently, had I known in advance. This simple one-day cancellation caused an entire ripple effect. Yes, flexibility, disappointment, and curve balls in general are a very normal part of life, however, it can be especially difficult and frustrating for a disabled person.

Additionally, being disabled often requires extra financial costs because one has to pay money for services he or she would normally be able to perform. I pay an extra thirty dollars per week to have my groceries delivered. I pay a service to do the pooper-scooping for my pets. I pay to have my apartment cleaned. I even used to pay my nephews to run errands for me. Sadly, it is part of the package.

Not only do we [disabled persons] feel badly about depending on others, we feel even worse if we believe that we somehow let them down. Although having the illness is not our fault, we often internalize it as a character flaw.

It is hard to make plans of any kind because we never know how we are going to feel on any given day. We could feel well in the morning and wind up in bed in the afternoon, or visa versa. I can't go out during the day, or be involved in a lot of activity at home, if I know I have evening plans. And, even refraining from that is no guarantee that I'll be able to execute said plans.

The worst part of it is feeling like we are letting family and friends down. There might be dishes in the sink, for long periods of time, because you are not up to washing them. This might cause you to feel like a bad mother or wife. Or if you are a man that can't take care of the yard work, it may make you feel like a disappointment. You might have special plans for your child's birthday party that you have to change, because you are not feeling well enough to host the event. There are other important events that you might miss like a friend's wedding, because you are in too much pain to attend.

The days spent in bed are filled with overwhelming guilt: You are missing a day in your family members' life. You are missing a day in your own life. You start estimating your worth less and less. *Who would even miss me if I were gone?* I still sometimes wonder.

Our attendance at church is a hit or miss. We can't commit to running a small group or Bible study, because we never know how we will feel on that day. It is difficult to tithe with such a limited income when you are out of work. That adds more guilt.

We internalize guilt if we believe we are genuinely letting our loved ones down. This causes isolation and loneliness. Seeing the disappointment in a child's face, or hearing it in your husband's voice, just magnifies the feeling that you are a bad person. *Nobody can count on me.* Eventually, we stop making plans and just hope for the best. Later we wonder why nobody calls us, and, as a result, we feel alienated. It is a vicious cycle.

The worst type of disappointment comes when we make every

attempt to do everything right: We eat a strict, healthy diet and exercise regularly. We take the proper medication, or other alternative therapies that seem to work for us. We get as much rest as possible before the event, and plan every detail so that things will run smoothly. Before the day arrives, we have invested a lot of time in preparation. That day finally arrives; we wake up in pain, and we know. At first we are in denial and try our best to manage. It doesn't take long before we realize, that despite all of our efforts and planning, it isn't going to work for us that day. It seems so unfair. We are disappointed in ourselves and we know we will be disappointing others.

The best we can do is explain our plight to our friends and family. Prepare them for the unknown. In the meantime, continue to prepare yourself with exercise, rest, and the proper pain medication to ensure good pain management. We want to have as many "near life experiences" as possible.

However, feeling left out causes the lonely monster to grow and swell like a tick. It highlights the fact that you are starkly different and have numerous needs. It fuels frustration.

Then there is that nasty lie that worms its way into your psyche. You already feel like a burden, but now you start to think that you are not liked, let alone loved.

"I know things are different, but couldn't you just say something that makes me feel involved in the family or event that is buzzing in the group?" Recently, I had to miss my cousin's wedding shower because it was on the second floor of a building. There was no elevator or handicapped bathroom available. At the time, I was disappointed with the people that planned the shower. I at least knew it was not my cousin's fault. Mary understood that I could not attend and why. It helped me realize that my disability doesn't always come to the forefront of people's minds. I was disappointed about the lack of consideration, but I also recognize that this event is about her, and not at all about me.

Sometimes, depending on the length of the disability, those in your life no longer remember to send cards, call you on the phone, or visit you at home. It's the calls you need most. You need to know that you are important, and valued, and that someone is thinking of you.

These are the times that we should lean on the Lord for comfort through reading scripture and praying. Satan can use that vulnerability to make you feel unloved and unwanted. You think that you are high maintenance and that nobody wants the burden. Even though we know better, we are often alone; these thoughts and feelings can creep in and destroy the fabric of our being. *Out of sight, out of mind.* We get an inflamed sense of rejection. Folks have busy lives and we know that. Yet, it still stings when our needs or feelings are not considered. It could be that you were not informed of a family event, or, by the time you were informed, you couldn't get the special transportation you need. It might happen that this special occasion was planned without considering your accessibility and/or limitations.

All these things that are trivial to an able-bodied person are very important considerations to a disabled person. To be thought of, and have your needs considered, is a sign of love and respect. Please remember: if these things do not happen, it does not mean that you are not loved. It might behoove you to remind your significant other of your needs, and where they are not being met. It is hard to not feel left out at times. However, our friends and family don't mean to hurt us. I know that my cousin has the kindest heart. I am the one who has to bend and adjust. If we dwell on it for too long, we can create unhealthy thought patterns.

Talking over these issues with a trusted friend or family member is so important. Holding in these feelings, can just foster other negative thoughts. I find that studying God's word puts me back into reality. I know that I have to talk to the Lord immediately when I am hurt or angry due to being left out. If I don't pray and read Scripture, my carnal mind takes over. I am no longer lead by the Holy Spirit. And I am empty.

CHAPTER 11

Back in the Saddle

I always kept a tube of lipstick on the kitchen table. My mother's oven had a strip of mirror on it. On the way out of the house, I would grab the lipstick, bend over to look in the mirror part of the oven, and happily apply my lipstick. On the way out one night, to put a deposit on new furniture we purchased, I grabbed my tube of lipstick and headed to the oven.

You have to understand that I have done this beauty ritual of mine for years. Years and years, and more years, until I did not even realize I was even doing it. All I remember, during that one ill-fated night: I stood at the oven with the lipstick in my hand. And I was screaming. I mean, screaming like I had never screamed before. When I had bent over, I felt this horrible "popping" feeling at the base of my spine. It was the most excruciating thing I ever felt. Both my husband and stepson came running when they heard my cries of pain. My husband wanted me to go lay down, but I thought that I would be okay and flatly refused. We went on to the furniture store. The entire time we were in the store, I was dying. I was trying to walk around like nothing was wrong. Eventually, I gave them the head nod towards the door, and we all knew it was time to go.

The next day, I woke up and I felt much better. I went happily along with my regular workday with no consequence. That evening I sat in on a colleague's class for two hours. I remember feeling relaxed but tired. When the class was over, I stood up and almost passed out. The pain at the base of my spine was epic. Nothing else has trumped it since. It felt as if a hot sword was shoved in my lower back, and the rest of my back muscles were on fire. I could not fathom walking to my car, but I did it anyway. I cried the entire walk there. I didn't even know if I could drive. All I wanted to do was get home, take some kind of medication, and get into bed.

The next day I stayed home from work. Our bed was downstairs, and there was a small powder room nearby as well. I was in the powder room trying to get off the toilet. I could not. I tried and I struggled and I cried to no avail. All of the sudden, I got the worst back spasms. Every time I tried to move, even slightly, it felt like somebody was sticking a spear in my lower spine. I was paralyzed with pain and with fear. I was stuck downstairs alone. I just started to scream. I screamed for my mother. My mother entered the powder room in seconds. She looked at me, and just put both of her arms under mine, and pulled me right up. Let me tell you, I was at least double her size. She was determined to get me up. Next, my mom almost carried me from the powder room back to my bed. I was hysterical. My poor mom didn't know what to do. I asked her just to put a pillow between my legs and get me a Motrin. I stayed in that bed for three days and nights. I tried to sit up multiple times. I just couldn't.

Every time I made the slightest attempt to sit up, those spasms came back, and my entire back locked up. After the third day of trying, I knew I had to go to the hospital. Buck wanted me to go before that, but I just keep thinking those sharp, stabbing dagger-like pains were going to just go away. They didn't. On a Friday night around dinner-time, Buck called the ambulance. We wound up back in the family ER again. They did the standard triage things, and gave me shots of morphine. I had x-rays done. The doctor wanted to discharge me like they do with most people experiencing back pain. "She can't ambulate," Buck said, "you can't send her home." Not only could I not walk, I still could not even sit up. Every time I tried, there was nothing but ear-piercing shrill screams coming from the depths of my soul.

The next few days were very interesting. I was pumped up with every drug imaginable. I was so high, that I could not remember phone conversations, or the people that came to visit. No matter what the medical team tried, nothing worked. They took MRIs, Cat Scans, and every test imaginable. At one point, they wanted to give me an epidural, but I had pressure sensitivity on my spine due to the fibromyalgia, so that was out of the question.

One day the doctor walked into my room and suggested, the last thing that we had not tried yet, a series of steroids called, a Medrol dose pack. I had never heard of this before. Apparently, that medication is very common and also inexpensive. Two days later, the physical therapists came back into my room. This time I could finally sit on the side of the bed. I yelled and cried, but I did it and that was all that mattered. I pushed through the pain because I could. The day after that I was on my feet. Within a few more days, I was walking down the hallway. It was slow but I could sit, stand, and walk again. Oh happy day!

I was out of work for a month. I had herniated a disc when I bent over the oven that day. I always called my doctor for a prescription of Medrol dose pack, if I felt back spasms coming on after that. Each and every time, those steroids did the trick by eliminating the inflammation, and ultimately, it quieted down the spasms. I have shared this secret with many people over the years. So many of them have come back to me, and thanked me, for sharing this with them. Does it work for everybody? No, of course not, but, luckily it worked for me.

CHAPTER 12

The Murder of a Marriage

Medication is another very sensitive issue. It is also highly debatable. A surplus of medication makes people more ill. Sometimes, the side effects can be worse than the condition for which we take them. I can't tell you how many medications I consumed that, subsequently, caused extreme intestinal distress. Other medications have given me the feeling of an out-of-the-body experience. The old adage, "If the disease doesn't kill you, the treatment will", can actually be true.

Another major issue people have with medication: addiction. The narcotic, Oxycodone, is used to relieve moderate to severe pain. It works by changing the way the brain, and nervous system, responds to pain. Oxycodone is highly addictive. Many doctors are now shying away from narcotic medications for fear of turning their patients into drug addicts. The drug, Methadone, is being used to serve as a pain killer as well. Methadone is synthetic heroin. It is what treatment facilities often use to assist heroine addicts to kick their habit. *Synthetic heroin is being used as a source of pain management?* I personally think that is frightening. Methadone is one drug, among many others, that can potentially injure an individual if it is not monitored appropriately.

These are all very confusing issues for the chronic pain sufferer. Because the doctors and pharmacists don't want to be sued, many do not believe in providing patients access to certain painkillers. Many patients do not like the feeling the drug produces while they are under its effects. I believe this is an individual choice. Many well-meaning family and friends—those that condemn their loved ones for taking narcotic medications—their opinions are unfair since they do not feel their pain.

Doctors should provide whatever pharmaceutical treatment works for the patient: steroids, medical marijuana, or narcotics, as radical as that sounds. Some folks will find another way to deal with their pain. But it is inhumane to deny the only course of treatment that works. It is inhumane to allow the patient to suffer.

Conversely, some people, suffering with chronic pain, pray in order to deal with their pain. The help received by going to God enables some people to relax, which, in turn, relaxes their muscles and eases their pain. I believe that many Americans tried prayer when dealing with their pain. Prayer is a critical tool used to cope with chronic illness. It is encouraging to know that we are not alone in the quest to deal with this physically, spiritually and emotionally crippling plight.

All Christians should give prayerful consideration to the various avenues of treatment. Although prayer is a source of power, to deal with the conditions suffered, I personally believe it should be used in conjunction with other therapies and not as a replacement for them. Some conditions left untreated can cause lasting damage.

※

Buck had a history of addiction. I knew this before I married him, but he had things under control. He even refused to take an aspirin for many years. However, Buck also had a bad back. This is when the circus began, during the back surgeries. Buck's first surgery was a spinal fusion of his lower back. They took a piece of his hip-bone, which was very painful, and used it in the fusion. Buck started taking narcotics. A few years later he had another fusion, this time in the thoracic area. Again, Buck started taking heavy medication. He eventually went to a pain management doctor, which was when he started on morphine. I could still kill that doctor right here and now.

Morphine took Buck down quickly. Everybody could see it but me, of course. He couldn't even keep his eyes open. He always told me that he was an insomniac, and that was why he was always so tired. Buck hunted down as much morphine as he could, and used every bit of it. I would often come home from work, and the house would be exactly as I left it. I would creep up the stairs slowly calling his name. I remember walking into the bedroom thinking, "Is today the day? Will this be the day I find Buck dead in bed?"

I tried my best to pretend none of this was even happening. I would go about my business, working, going out with my friends, and even visiting my mom. This was too much to face. I convinced myself that everything would work out. I figured that since we went through tough times before, and we got through them, we would be fine. This too, shall pass.

Eventually, it got so bad that Buck decided to get a morphine pump implanted to end his addiction. I went to the hospital with Buck and watched this, no less than historic, event. I watched him start to detoxify, and throw up green bile. It was horrible. I don't think that either Buck or I realized the gravity of the situation. He thought this was the answer. He would not have to depend on pills anymore. We both knew that it was a drastic measure, but something had to be done. One week later, one of his stitches from the morphine pump surgery got infected. We were back the next day, for an emergency surgery, to have the morphine pump removed. That had to be the worst thing I ever witnessed. Buck detoxified so badly that I thought he might die. He shook violently, and sweat poured off of him like a moving river. He hallucinated and cried and begged for mercy. The staff members at Fox Ridge Cancer Center in Philadelphia, where Buck had his surgery, let us stay in a patient lounge so that we could be together. They came and gave him as much medicine as they could; but, it was still so bad. I held him, and rocked him, and wiped his wet body, and covered him with blankets. Part of me was dying with him there on that small sofa, as he crawled into a fetal position.

CHAPTER 13

In the Muck with Buck

On November 7, 2001, Buck got arrested for not paying child support. We had seen this coming because our neighbors mentioned that the sheriff's department had been to our house on several occasions. I could never understand why he avoided his responsibility like the plague.

I was not that concerned because I thought that Buck would just be in jail for perhaps a week or two, and then he would be released. I drove to the Lindenwold police station the day he was arrested. Buck was crying; he was crying hard. In fact, he was weeping as if somebody just died. I wiped his tears, and reminded him that I was the one that should be crying. One week later, I went to the bank to close my mother's bank account, and take the money to the nursing home. After filling out the withdrawal form, I sat at the banker's desk waiting to get $8,000 in my hand. "There is only $1.98 in this account," the woman behind the desk said. I laughed and insisted that there must be some kind of mistake.

Then the bank teller allowed me to look at a check that had recently been written against the account. It was paid to my husband's name, and my name was forged in his handwriting. At that point, the room starting spinning . I felt like I would pass out. Buck emptied my mother's bank account! The banker proceeded to tell me that she saw my husband's truck quite often at the drive-thru. I felt my knees going weak, and thought that I might fall onto the floor. *This can't be happening*, I thought. *How could this have happened? How could he have stolen my mother's money?*

I have never felt waves of shock in my life as I did that day. I felt as though somebody had just dropped a grand piano on my head. My mind was racing. My heart was beating out of my chest. I felt numb. I couldn't think straight. I walked out of the bank completely stunned and crying hysterically. I found myself behind the wheel driving. I don't remember going from the bank to the nursing home. I was crying to the point of almost hyperventilating. They took me right back into the office. I was gasping for air while trying to explain to the administrator what happened. All my mother's money was gone without my knowledge. The people at Cadbury were very nice to me. They said that I should leave and go home because I was so upset. They asked if my husband was in jail, and I said yes. This satisfied them. It was true, but he wasn't in jail for stealing my mother's money. I drove directly to my cousin's house. I will never forget the feeling I had. Or, should I say, lack of feeling. I was in shock. Nothing seemed real. My cousin was doing her thing of being totally calm and not responding to my reactions. She simply asked me what happened, and expressed herself softly saying, "Oh my", and, "Is that right?" I had some friends that wanted to find him, and run him over with their car. Nobody could believe it.

The next day, I went to my own bank to see what damage was done there. There was NO money in my account. They were also very nice to me, and ordered a copy of all cancelled checks from my account. I could feel God with me the entire time I was there. I knew the folks at the bank did not realize the scope—the sheer magnitude of what had transpired—but I did. I went to pay my mortgage payment with the money from my most recent check. A voice came into my head; it reminded me to check the equity wrap. I knew it was God's voice. I would never have even thought about the equity wrap because we never used it. I kept thinking, "Oh God no, please don't tell me!" Yep, we had a $20,000.00 equity loan against the house. Gone...all gone! Buck had done it!

The next three days were among the worst of my life. *How did I not know? How could I have trusted him? How could he do this? Did he know what he was doing? Did I even know him? Was he just play-*

ing me all these years? It was like torture. The person who was my beloved became the thief who stole everything from me. *What was happening?*

In the meantime, I was missing a lot of work and pressure mounted there too. I felt like I couldn't show my face, or even lift my head off the pillow. There was stuff to get done, therefore, I was not allowed the luxury of having a nervous breakdown. In the days and weeks that followed, bills started coming in. I never worried about the bills because Buck would write them out, and bring them to me to sign. It was all taken care of, so I thought. When I started opening these bills, I found I owed thousands of dollars. But these bills were paid, I thought. *Wrong!* Buck wrote them out, but never mailed them. Once I started searching, I found checks I had written, to pay bills, hidden all over the house. Obviously, they were never mailed. Shock number two: Due to Buck's theft, I was forced to file bankruptcy. It was humiliation personified.

During this time, my friends gathered around me like an army of dolphins protecting their young. People came over and changed the locks. They cleaned out mountains of trash left by Buck. Different friends drove me places. They mapped out a plan that every night I would go to somebody's house for dinner. My colleagues from the Criminal Justice Academy at work made a call to the prosecutor's office and they came to my house and took a statement. I was stoic. I was a robot just going through the motions. My family and friends held me up when I couldn't stand. It was truly amazing. The Lord was sending out the troops in droves to help me.

Financially, things just kept getting worse. The waves of disbelief continued. Apparently, I had no car insurance for the new car I bought eight months prior. When I attempted to get insurance, I found out that I had no driver's license. There were little surprises like this on an almost constant basis. All my gold jewelry was gone. My mother's wedding and engagement rings were also missing. I knew the car that I had just bought, would have to go back. I called the dealership, crying, and asked them to come and repossess my car after I left for work, since I could not watch my dream car being towed away.

Suddenly, I got a burst of energy and I did not know where it came from. I was on a mission. I was going to gather all the evidence I needed to make a case against Buck. This was something I had to do to prevent my mother from being discharged from the best nursing home in South Jersey. I got all the checks from my mother's account, my account, and the equity wrap that had been forged, and put them in a binder. I had to go to several different police departments to file charges, and I got copies of all the police reports. My binder started growing daily. By the time we went to court, the binder was six inches thick. But I had a new mantra: In order to keep my mother in, I had to lock my husband up.

This all took a big piece of my heart, and my soul, and completely stomped out all my dreams. My mom was in a nursing home, my husband was in jail, and my stepson was gone from my life. Thankfully, I still had my dogs.

CHAPTER 14

Ouch

I plummeted into a deep depression. The love of my life was gone. He lied to me, robbed me, and sliced my heart and soul into little pieces. I was functioning on autopilot. Nothing mattered. I was just getting by. I would lie around wondering which bridge I should climb to jump to my death. As I was driving, I would go pole picking. "Humm, that's a good one there, won't hurt other people, just myself." I would wonder how fast I would have to drive in order to die.

These were the dark nights of the soul. The only things that kept me from truly self-destructing were my dogs. I could not leave them with anybody else. Days turned into weeks, and weeks turned into months. I was having a very difficult time paying the bills. The house my mother worked so hard to maintain was falling down around me. I felt like I was living in Herman Munster's house. I called my friends to help me get the house back in shape. One of my friends suggested that I sell the house, pay off all my bills, and start over in an apartment. I had never even considered that. How could I think about giving up my inheritance? This is my parent's home. Yet, the more I thought about it, the more I thought it was a good idea. I took the advice, and made the decision to get the house ready to sell.

Once again, people came in by the droves to help me. My family, friends, neighbors and coworkers all showed up. Every weekend, for six months, a team of people came over and performed different tasks. They ripped up the rugs, power washed the house, and packed my life into boxes. For me, this was an exercise in, total and complete, emotional torture once again. I was going through my mother's entire life, and my own, which was very painful for me. Every time I would see something that triggered a memory, it was like somebody shot me with a gun. I had to keep going. I could not have all of those folks over at my house, helping me, while I just sat there sucking my thumb, which is what I wanted to do. I had to make the decisions about what stayed, and what got trashed. I remember being so exhausted that I thought I would surely die.

During that time, I started experiencing intense pain in my hip. I thought it might be from all of the-running-around. I could not sleep at night because of the pain. Many other things were going on that needed my attention, so my health was on the bottom of the list of things to worry about. I started looking for apartments. This was an event in itself. Very few apartments would accept dogs. I had both Geordie and Neelix, and neither of them were going anywhere. I could not lose another thing. I refused. Many of my friends advised me to get rid of Neelix, because he was a pit-bull. Despite the fact that Neelix was my problem child, he was also was my joy.

My realtor, Crystal, was a family friend. She worked very hard looking for a buyer for my house. I had to sell the house "as is", which also decreased the value. I was disappointed with the money I made on the house, but very grateful to Crystal for getting me though a settlement.

I found a high-rise apartment complex in Collingswood, New Jersey that looked promising. The building seemed secure and I would be about a mile away from my cousin's house, which was great! I quickly accepted the fact that this was my new home. There were plenty of dogs, of all breeds, including pit-bulls that resided there. I could not have been happier. This was much better than a tent under the nearest bridge. That is where I would have ended up, because I wasn't giving up my dogs. The move was a difficult. None of us adapted very well in the beginning. It took a long time to adjust to living in a high-rise apartment building. Once I was in the apartment, all the support I was used to getting was gone. I was a high maintenance person, and often, I felt like a burden to those who were closest to me. Besides, after the past six months of working on my house, my friends needed a break. It was around this time, that I decided to stop asking for help. I decided to do things on my own. That didn't go very well at all

CHAPTER 15

The Dark Days

Have courage for the great sorrows of life and patience
for the small ones; and when you have laboriously
accomplished you daily task, go to sleep in peace,
God is awake. —*Victor Hugo*

A year later, I found myself barely able to function at work. Standing up was very difficult. I had to back my chair up to the wall and pull myself up. I accompanied this movement with my repertoire of pain noises. I walked like Quasimodo. I noticed that my left foot was becoming numb and slowly turning out to the left. I was hanging on by a very thin thread. I stopped getting my own lunch in the cafeteria, because I could not navigate through the crowd. My colleagues would run my errands for me. I had to walk my dogs up and down two flights of stairs in order to take them out. I went right to bed after walking them. The pain was unbearable. I started to wonder how much more I could take of this. I knew I had to keep going at work, but as far as life at home was concerned, I was done. I could not clean, cook, or do laundry. I did not have the strength and I could not bear the pain. All of the pain in my muscles—my back, my feet and legs, and especially my hip—debilitated me on a regular basis. It was no secret that I was suffering. My family and friends did what they could to help me. In reality, when I look back at that time, I should have had a professional caretaker, and more assisted living equipment to make my life easier. I really believed that having a wheelchair was for folks a lot worse off than me.

One day, mid-February 2008, I told my coworkers that I felt like I was getting a cold and I might not be in the next day. Little did I realize, that would be my last day, of a twenty-year employment, at Camden Community College. I became very ill. I could not breathe. I could barely walk from the bedroom to the bathroom. My friends took me to the Emergency Room because I could not catch my breath. It was terrible. Every Monday, for five weeks, I wound up on my doctor's doorstep. She became very worried because my lips were blue and the illness lingered for so long. My doctor pulled some strings with a colleague of hers who was a lung specialist.

I have to say, in all my years, I never had a better doctor than Dr. Bermingham. He was so kind and thorough—a phenomenal doctor and an amazing person. He treated me with such respect and dignity. I began to have faith in the medical community again. On my first visit, I was asked to walk up and down the hallway for as long and as fast as I could. Subsequently, I could not catch my breath when I was done. I wound up in the hospital due to my unsuccessful stroll down the corridor. They kept me in there all night. The next morning, a nurse said that I was going to be discharged because all my tests results were normal. "What about the blood clot that they diagnosed earlier," I asked. I called my friend Deborah and she came right over. It was during that time, as I laid helplessly on a gurney, I got the call from the college that my contract was not going to be renewed. I was done. My employment at Camden County College would end in July, which was three months away. I was in a state of shock. I just could not believe it. I was one of the last people to go, but I wasn't ready for it. *What will I do? How will I survive?* It was like a bomb went off in my mind. All I could do was lay there on the gurney and cry.

Luckily, I saw Dr. Bermingham's colleague, and told him what was going on. His entire facial expression changed when I mentioned a blood clot. He went right to the phone. He came back to my bed and apologized. He said that, yes, I did have a blood clot, and that I would be admitted to the hospital. I was in the hospital for one week. I had to be taught to give myself a blood thinner: a shot in the stomach. After I learned, I was discharged.

A month later I woke up and my foot was very swollen. My leg was also red and felt like it was on fire. I called my endocrinologist who told me to go right to the hospital. When I walked into the ER, they took my vital signs, and I was rushed back and given a gurney inside a small room. Thankfully, I was given oxygen as well. Finally, my breathing improved. The doctor said my blood-oxygen was too low; I was in critical condition. Once again, I was in the hospital for a week. Right before I was released, I had to walk down the hallway while they measured my blood-oxygen level. The technician told me to go back to the room. Apparently, my blood-oxygen was down to 80% from that brief slow stroll down hospital corridor. I was ordered to go home with oxygen. Oh, no, I thought. Enough is enough. I can't add this to my list too.

Early the next morning, there was a knock at my door. It was a respiratory therapist coming to drop off the oxygen. There were small, mini tanks with five pounds of oxygen, and other big tanks on wheels, and one, huge contraption that apparently made air if I needed it. I was overwhelmed and disgusted. *I'm 48 years old and look at me. I might as well check into my mother's nursing home.*

CHAPTER 16

Quicksand

Courage is not simply one of the virtues,
but the form of every virtue at the testing point.
—C. S. Lewis

The loss of my mom, followed by my dog, Geordi, a few months later, was overwhelming. Even though my anti-depressant, Lexapro, was increased, the sheer magnitude of those losses stayed with me. They drained me both physically and mentally.

I can't walk, I can't stand, and I can't breathe. I can't get my own meals, I can't take the dog out, I can't clean or do laundry. I can't get to the store. I just can't.

Eventually, I stopped driving because the walk to the car was too far. I could not do it any longer. My life had come to a complete stand still.

My bedroom became my refuge. I knew that as long as I was in bed, I could manage the pain. I was never really comfortable. I had a deep, yet dull, ache in my hip that never went away. It hurt to move, and trying to roll over was an event in itself. I would get horrific Charlie-horses in my calves, as well as my thighs, that would push me over the edge. Those muscle spasms happened several times a night, and would last for what seemed like hours.

My cousin Mary, and her sons, basically saved my life during that time. If we did not live close to each other, I might have ended up in a nursing home. My cousin drove the boys to my apartment everyday to walk the dog in the morning, and at night. She did all of my shopping. Her sons did my laundry. I would sit and wait for them to come through the door. Mary would come in my room, and sit on my bed, and hold my hand. She spoke such comfort to me so often. Mary shined with optimism and hope, and she gave me reasons to keep fighting. She would prepare my food and put it next to my bed. Mary did everything. During this time, my cousin became my best friend.

When I was alone, I began to think that there was nobody left in the world but me. I could hear people outside, but I would feel so jealous that they were out in the sun and clean air. I never knew what the weather was because I couldn't reach the curtains. I never really cared as long as the temperature in my room was warm enough, or cool enough, depending on the season. I was becoming isolated, both mentally and physically, from the rest of the world.

Neelix became a very important part of my life. My dog actually became my life-line. He was with me all the time. He stayed on the bed with me. Often, he just stared at me. I would scream for him when I was having extreme difficulty. He was a living, breathing entity with which I shared my space. I would lay my hand on him just to feel him breathing, or just to feel the warmth of his body.

During this time, I really started to talk out loud to Neelix. I told him everything, the good, the bad, and the ugly. Sometimes, he would just stare at me; other times, he would wag his tail. I wondered if he hated me because of this pseudo existence we had. I apologized to him. I was sorry that he was stuck with me as an owner, because he was such a good dog.

It was during this time that the sleeplessness hit me as well. It wasn't that slumber would not come, but that I could not sleep at night. I would start tossing and turning around 2:00 am. Television became very important to me during this time. I loved to watch both QVC and HSN, and order the things I thought I deserved: Pocket books, jewelry, bedding, and the list went on.

This was an angry time for me. I had become restless and bitter. Why was this happening to me? What had I done in life that was so bad? Why?

I never envisioned my life ending up like this! Where are they all?

All the people that I dedicated my life to, before this illness, have abandoned me now during my time of need. Don't they know how I am suffering here? Oh, while I was healthy enough to do things for them, that was all right. Now that I am on my back, barely able to move, where are they? This was not even near the truth. In reality, I had a sea of supportive friends. I felt so isolated and alone. This was totally irrational thinking.

I did not realize it then, but I was grieving. I was letting go of the life I once had. I had been so lucky to know so many wonderful people. I was blessed to have worked with the greatest people on the planet, and gifted with the most amazing group of people as friends. It was obvious things were going to change now. How could I let them go? My friends were all worried about me, and they would call all the time. I tried to do the best I could to cover my anguish. I felt so disconnected from the rest of the world.

I became severely depressed. I started to think that I could not take this anymore. Life was not worth living with this illness and pain. I was worthless, just the shell of the person I once was. I stopped bathing, brushing my hair, or bothering to get dressed. I wanted to die. I would ask God to please take me in my sleep. I would look at some of the medication that I had, and wonder if I had enough to kill me. I never considered killing myself any other way. It would be too messy. With the pills, I would just go to sleep and float away. Nobody would miss me, really, because I had been gone for a while. They would all understand. Then I would think it through for a moment, and my eyes always fell on Neelix. *Who would take my boy? He is such a nervous wreck, how would he survive with anybody else. Nobody understands him like I do. He can't take a lot of yelling and noise. I just can't up and leave Neelix.*

My thoughts fell on my cousin also. I thought that either Mary, or one of her boys, would be the ones to find me. How horrible that would be for them. I could never possibly put them through that. I thought about my dearest friends, and how they would feel, and how sad they would be. They would be sad, and disappointed, and possibly angry that I took the suicide route. No, that wasn't an option. At least until the next time my thoughts looped around the same morbid process.

It was during this deep desperation, that I started to argue with God. I mean that they were knock-down, drag-out arguments. I would look up and yell at the top of my lungs, "Why???" *Why is this happening to me? Was I so bad? What did I ever do to deserve enduring such misery? I have asked you for forgiveness, can't you hear me? Dear God in heaven, help me! Are you there? I know you are there, yet why am I going through this? You are my rock and my salvation. Why aren't you helping me now? What is the reason for this? Please take me home so this suffering will end, I beg you.*

I could feel God's presence. I knew He was there. But He did not choose to answer me the way I thought he should. I kept waiting for this big turnaround, a miracle, a healing. Nothing. Neelix and I, in the bed, day after day and night after night, was all that was left of my life. Those arguments with God continued on a regular basis, and I rather enjoyed them. I felt good about them. I knew God heard me.

Close to a year passed. I started to watch some Christian broadcasting on TV. Most of the time it made me feel resentful when everybody seemed to be getting healed but me. One night, I heard that we were supposed to thank God for all things. I thought about this long and hard. The announcer said whether things are good or bad, thank Him because he is going to use them for his glory. How can I possibly thank Him for this? I thought. It would be too ridiculous. It's absurd! Thank Him for this chronic illness and pain?

One day, as I sat on the corner of my bed, I yelled," Thank you, alright? "Did you hear me?" I said, "I'm thanking you because that is what I'm supposed to do. I don't want to do it and I think it's crazy to thank you for torment, but if that is what I am told to do, then I will do it." Some way, some how, I started to learn the lesson of obedience. It was in that moment when I had a moment of clarity: God was for me, not against me.

CHAPTER 17

Clarity

I started to thank God regularly. In doing that, my prayer life developed again. It took time, but instead of arguing with God, I started talking to him. I could feel his presence during our time together. I could feel the touch of the Holy Spirit on me. This was the turning point. This was when my life, once again, took on meaning. I still complained and pleaded to God, but I praised him and thanked Him as well. There was a light that started to grow inside me. I knew that I was not alone. Jesus was always by my side, helping me, guiding me. I was just too spiritually blind to see it.

One day as I meditated, I thought about Jesus in the Garden before his walk to the cross. Scripture notes—in Matthew chapter 26, verse 38—that Jesus told His companions in the Garden, "My soul is overwhelmed with sorrow to the point of death. Stay here and keep watch with me." I had an epiphany that Jesus *knows* what it is like to feel despair. He, himself, felt it. I was NOT alone and never would be again.

In Matthew 26:39, Jesus prayed, "My Father, if it is possible, may this cup be taken from me. Yet not as I will, but as you will." I realized that I had not committed some unforgivable sin for which I was being punished. God, in is His infinite wisdom, knows the purpose of this even though I do not. He was not ignoring me, or abandoning me, or leaving me to shrivel up and die. This gave me such blessed hope. Then, I also realized that God on earth felt the physical pain of the crucifixion. God allowed Jesus, his son, to suffer that terrible, painful death. All the agony that Jesus went through was for my salvation. My sins, the world's sins, were forgiven and suffering was allowed in order to further the kingdom of heaven. I knew this was true for many years, but suddenly it took on new meaning. It did not mean that my life would not continue to be challenging, it just meant that I would not be alone through it. God knew every painful step I took. This brought me such comfort. I started to look at things totally different. I can't say that I turned into a suffering martyr, because I did not. Did my complaining continue? Of course it did. However, now I knew somebody heard it and understood it. Did I cry to be released from the affliction? Yep, I did that too. I also knew that there was a reason for it all. I just didn't know what it was.

During this time, I applied for Social Security (Disability). I was awarded benefits within two months of applying. No attorney— no denials—it was the Lord preparing me for good things to come. This was a miracle. But, my trials were not over yet.

CHAPTER 18

The Knife

I heard of a doctor—his office was about an hour away—he did not mind operating on heavy patients. "This is too good to be true," I thought. I made an appointment right away. My friend Peg drove down with me. The doctor assured me that he has operated on patients bigger than me. He was very personable. We all agreed that a second hip replacement, on the left side, would be difficult, no doubt. We discussed what life would be like once I healed. There really wasn't an alternative; I needed to have this surgery. I was so excited.

I knew that all my problems would be over once my hip was replaced. My left foot would start walking straight, and there will be no more back issues to worry about. The entire problem is my hip. *No worries, I will prevail. Victory will be mine. God will take care of everything.*

The day finally arrived for my surgery. My friend Eric accompanied me. I was so nervous. I gave a little speech to Eric, regarding Neelix, in the event that something went horribly wrong during the operation. I also left my final wishes with my cousin. They both cited as many positive affirmations as they could. I was skeptical of a positive outcome, because I remember how things manifested after my first hip replacement. People who have not undergone that type of surgery are clueless. I knew it would not be easy. I also knew that the Lord would be carrying me through the entire process. I closed my eyes.

I woke up to see Eric, sitting in a chair, in front of me. "You look exhausted," I said. He laughed, since I was the one coming out of surgery. Eric tried to explain that the doctor had a difficult time operating because my bones were soft or something. But, I wasn't comprehending it. To me it just felt like he was babbling, and I remember that he didn't look happy. The next thing I knew, the surgeon came and put his hand on my shoulder. He looked narrowly into my eyes and said, "You were the hardest surgery of my career." *How lovely. That is just what I needed to know right now.* Later, the surgeon also explained that I had waited so long, that my hip had almost fused together. That was the reason for the excruciating pain.

I remember the first time I stood up, my leg felt beyond heavy. "What the heck is this?" I wondered. "I don't remember this happening with my first hip replacement." Everything came into light when I tried to walk. My left foot was not having it! "No way", it screamed, "don't even bother." I would stare at my foot, and leg, and demand it to move, but nah, nope, nada—nothing.

CHAPTER 19

Acute Acuteness

Rehabilitation was hell. At first I only dragged my foot. I could not pick it up at all. I couldn't even feel it on the floor. The physical therapists would literally walk my foot for me. One therapist would pick up the front of my foot, while the other would go behind me. They both proceeded to mimic the action of a walking foot. My foot mocked them. And me. It was apparent that it did not want to cooperate.

I was diagnosed with something called "drop foot", which was one of the common side effects of the surgery. It had to do with damaged nerves, which caused a form of neuropathy. For some people, it was temporary, and, for others, it was permanent. Only time would tell what the case would be for me.

The therapist pushed me to increase the distance I walked. And then she pushed me some more. It was so amazingly hard to walk just a few steps. I could not feel the floor, nor could I pick up my foot at all. My left leg felt like it weighed five hundred pounds. I could barely make it to the commode, and I couldn't get my leg up into the bed by myself. I would be in bed, and totally exhausted, by 3:00 pm. The bad pain started around 7:00 pm. My foot would start to feel like it was on fire. Suddenly this pain would start, that would have me weeping as quietly as possible, but crying in pain none-the-less. They started to increase my meds, which helped, but never enough. I still continued to cry every night. Eventually, they made me a special brace for my leg and foot that was supposed to help me walk better. *Greaaattt, another thing for me to try and lift, I thought.* The therapy was grueling. I was NOT allowed to give up. I was so tired. It was hard for folks to visit because the rehab was an hour away. My friend Milly came as much as she could, and she called every day. Most friends could only come once because of the distance. It was also difficult for my cousin. Eric visited several times and brought his grand-daughter, Saige. She is an amazing kid who would put the biggest smile on my face. I instantly felt better when I saw Eric walk through the door holding Saige's hand.

I saw the Lord dancing into that therapy room everyday, and it made my heart swell. In between my own therapy, I would watch the other patients. It was a huge, open room where you could see what as going on around you. I saw all kinds of people there. Some recovering patients waltzed through the therapy, and others, like me, were sweating and struggling. The thing that impressed me: we all struggled. I was the most impressed by the brain-injured folks for some reason. I knew I was watching miracles.

It was a very positive environment. The patients often cheered each other on. I remember when I took my first ten steps, there was a group of people watching me and cheering. I did the same thing for others who came after me. I started watching the miracle of healing with people—not able to even stand up on their own—now they were taking steps. My eyes would fill, almost every day, with the tears of gratitude and amazement. There, folks were accomplishing phenomenal things.

People would start therapy slumped over, almost drooling on themselves, due to their injuries. Day by and day, and week by week, I could see them improve. Soon, a healthy, smiling face replaced their grey colored skin and pain-filled eyes. I thanked God every day for the progress I saw with others.

It became apparent that I was not ready to go home and needed a sub-acute rehab (sub-acute rehabilitation is suited to patients that cannot tolerate more than three hours of physical therapy each day). The day before, I was transferred to the new facility; I was treated for cellulites due to the worsening Lymphedema. I woke up abruptly with a terrible burning in my chest. As a precaution, I was sent to the ER where they ran a lot of tests on my heart. This was merely a precautionary measure on their part. I was released from the ER with no damage to my heart at all. The next day, I made the long trek to a facility near home.

I was so happy to be nearer to home. I was staying in the same town where several of my closest friends lived, so I knew I would see them. I spent the following day settling into the new facility. At about 4:00 pm, I felt this weird lump in my lip. I called the nurse and explained that there was something wrong with my lip. She said that she had a feeling that my lips might swell, and that she would check back with me later. When she came back, both of my lips were swollen. She gave me two Benadryl and announced that she would come back in an hour. I called my best friend to let her know what was going on. It was obvious that I was having an allergic reaction.

An hour later, the nurse supervisor came in, looked at me, and told me she was calling an ambulance. She kept asking me if I could breathe. All I knew was that my lips were getting more swollen by the minute. In fact, I could see them. When I looked down, I could actually see them! Two of my friends met me at the hospital. I noticed everybody staring at me when the ambulance brought me in. I thought it was because I had these micro-braid extensions for hair. Heads were turning to stare at me. I had no a clue why I fascinated everyone. We, my friends, the nurses, other sickos, chatted for a while, but it was getting increasingly harder to talk. In fact, it was getting down right painful. They found great humor in calling me Octo-mom. I was not aware at the time, but my entire face had blown up: my eyes were almost shut and I was becoming unrecognizable. I was given a needle and sent back to the rehab. It took days before my face looked normal again. The hospital told me that if I ever took that antibiotic, Clindamycin, again, I would die before I got to the hospital, because I am highly allergic.

I was in the sub-acute rehab for a month. I did improve slightly in there. I could lift my leg into the bed and I could walk longer distances. That's about it though. I was still in bad shape when I was sent home. It took months before I could do anything for myself without assistance.

I had to purchase many things to help me with my recovery: a shower bench, a raised toilet seat, and walker with a seat on it, among other things. Even though I was on disability, I had exhausted my bank account.

CHAPTER 20

The Rise and Fall of My Extremities

My feet have been swollen for as long as I can remember. I think I popped out of the womb with swollen legs and feet. I don't ever remember looking down and seeing an ankle. I was so used to it, that my friends and I used to call my feet, and legs, "The Pumpkins and the Tree-Trunks". My family called them "cankles". If I was sick with a fever, and in bed for a few days, the swelling would go down and I would actually take a picture of my feet. I would be so proud of that picture too. I longed for my feet and legs to stay that way, but, as soon as I was back up walking on them, the swelling would commence. Once again, the pumpkins and tree-trunks would expand out of my shoes.

There came a time—I don't remember when, and I don't know why—the edema on my feet and legs started to intensify. I could do nothing but climb into my recliner when I got home, because I felt so uncomfortable. My skin was starting to stretch. The summertime was always worse with increased swelling. This new, "attack of the 50 foot woman", routine my feet were doing became unmanageable. I wasn't able to tolerate it as I had for so many years.

A colleague suggested that I go to a vascular surgeon. I discovered that I had primary Lymphedema in my feet and legs. I researched Lymphedema on the computer and saw pictures of people with a one-hundred-pound extremity: image after image of the grossest thing I have ever seen. I was told there was nothing to be done to cure this condition. The vascular surgeon prescribed compression boots that hooked up to a pump. I had to use the compression boots three times a day for an hour. It managed the problem initially, but later did nothing to contract the size of my feet and legs.

Lymphedema was not my only physical ailment.

Due to the complications of my hip replacement, other issues besides drop foot, and neuropathy, became apparent. The lymphedema in my feet and legs seemed to explode after my hip surgery. In order to accommodate my new found puffiness, I had to purchase a man's size 13, 6x sneaker. The edema was really bad and painful as well. At times, it just felt like the skin on my feet would tear and my feet would hulk-ify. Due to the hip replacement, my lymph nodes were not draining the protein, that collected in my lower extremities, correctly. This fluid was building up, and thanks to gravity, it deposited in my feet and calves.

I heard of a local Lymphedema clinic through the Virtua In Motion Outpatient Rehabilitation Department. The occupational therapist there was named Kathy. Kathy called and informed me of all the necessary items I needed to start treatment. I was shocked at all the different types of wraps, and their different sizes, I had to purchase. I also needed a specific type of foam to complete the wrapping process. I had to purchase two cast boots in order to be able to walk after being wrapped. I wondered if I would look like a person from outer space after each therapy session.

On my first consultation with Kathy, I was scared to death. Kathy was very stern, and reminded me of a drill sergeant. *I can't do this again,* I thought to myself. I had no choice. I could not continue to exist with my "tree trunks and pumpkins" in full bloom so to speak. There were too many other things to worry about beside the Lymphedema.

I still could not drive since my hip replacement surgery. I took the "Access Link" Bus to my appointments. "Access Link" is the local bus service tor the handicapped. I would be gone six hours a day for a one-hour appointment. The bus often collected me hours before my appointment, and then not for several hours after when coming home. If that was not the case, then the rides might be exceptionally long. It was another exercise in endurance, one that made me very miserable.

Treatment for Lymphedema included a specific set of massages before the wrapping would commence. These massages were to assist the lymph node drainage in different places on the body. The bandages were applied directly after the massage. I would lay on the therapy table and Kathy would complete the massage. I remember thinking how good that felt and fell asleep quite a few times.

It was the wrapping that was problematic. In the beginning, my left leg was so heavy that Kathy would need assistance lifting it while wrapping. She would use the different layers of wraps, and tape one to another, while working her way from my foot to the top of my calf. I could handle the right foot and leg with no problem. It was when Kathy would wrap my left leg, that all the agony would begin. Day after day, I would cry as my left leg was wrapped. The nerve behind my knee, that often irritated me, entered into a full on war with my pain sensors. As time went on, this pain diminished.

Kathy was a very delightful and intelligent lady. We would talk about a variety of different subjects. I found my therapist to be a kind soul who always had a suggestion on how to improve any situation. That rehabilitation facility was over-crowded and over-booked. Kathy often arrived early, stayed late, and didn't take a lunch break.

Kathy helped me acquire the compression stockings that I needed upon completion of my therapy. The Cancer Society donated a pair of Jobs Stockings. I was thrilled. Sadly, despite all the assistance that was provided to me, I did not have success with those stockings. My insurance would no longer pay for any Lymphedema therapy, and Kathy had to move on to new patients. I went to Kathy two to three times a week for over a year.

I was very sad when I was discharged from Kathy's care. I felt abandoned and alone. I was so afraid that my legs would "re-inflate". I had to deal with this situation on my own. Although she had trained another friend of mine to help me wrap my legs, it was not successful. My friend did not feel comfortable, and did not want to continue with the process.

I talked to another friend, Mary Anne, who also suffered from the same condition. I was very upset because I knew if I didn't do something soon, all the progress that I had made working with Kathy would be for nothing. Mary Anne casually mentioned that she went for therapy at an office out of University of Pennsylvania Hospital in Cherry Hill, minutes from my new apartment.

This is where I met my next Lymphedema therapist, Rebecca. My first appointment with Rebecca was very much like my first appointment with Kathy. Rebecca was scary. She took a brief glance at my feet and knew that the stockings I had were not going to work for me. Rebecca began to grill me about how I would maintain my progress after we completed therapy. She was convinced that she could get my feet and legs down to where they needed to be, but spelled out everything it would take to maintain it. She told me there was no point in starting therapy if I couldn't provide what it takes to keep the condition at bay.

Rebecca recited the expenses of all the supplies that I would need to buy to start therapy, and the garments I would need to purchase afterwards. This list tripled, in price, the one that I needed from my former therapist. The supplies alone would cost slightly more than $400.00. The night-time garments I would need cost at least $500.00 per leg, and the custom made stockings I needed cost around $200.00 per leg. My head started swimming. I remember thinking, *You gotta be kidding me! How am I going to do this?*

All of a sudden, as if I was reading a script, I looked at Rebecca and I said, "I'm not worried, I'll find a way." Rebecca looked me in the eye with all the seriousness she could muster. I remember thinking, *man alive, she doesn't want any new patients, does she?* Mary Anne spoke so highly of Rebecca. I was trying to see those qualities on my first visit. But it would take me more than one visit to get to know her as a therapist and a person.

I was transferring from my COBRA insurance to Medicare in August of 2010, so we agreed that I should wait to start therapy. I would keep off my feet as much as possible, and stay out of the heat, until we could get started. In October I ordered the $400.00 worth of supplies I needed, and I was off to Penn Therapy and Fitness on Route 70 in Cherry Hill, New Jersey. I drove three minutes from my house, a minimum of four times per week, for a two hour session. Later, our therapy sessions just involved wrapping.

Virtua In Motion Rehabilitation Department and Penn Therapy were two very different rehabilitation facilities, with very different philosophies. Rebecca had her own private office that was quite large. There was a large therapy table in the office. I would schedule two hour blocks of time for massage and wrap therapy. Their actual therapy techniques varied, which caused me a great deal of concern initially. I came to the conclusion that it didn't matter how they did it, as long as it worked.

Rebecca was a breath of fresh air. She turned out to be very personable as well as professional. I had the utmost confidence in Rebecca. She had a very hardy laugh and could be quite humorous. We took turns story telling during the therapy sessions, and would often laugh very hard. I was relaxed when working with Rebecca as well.

I found out about the Marilyn Westbrook garment fund and took all the steps I needed to apply way before our therapy ended. My therapy ended when my Circiad night –time garments arrived, and Rebecca measured them and taught me how to use them correctly.

For a year, everything was going along nicely. I made an appointment with Rebecca when the strap on my Circaid garment started to fray and twist out of shape. It no longer secured the garment in the proper place. Surprisingly, Circaid agreed to send a new pair of garments. However, that is when the trouble began.

The reason for the new Circaid garments not working is still a mystery. There has been much speculation as to a change in material used to make the garments, and many other assorted hypothesizes— the bottom line, the garments didn't work. It was as if I was wearing nothing at all. My feet and legs once again swelled to the point that I had to wear my men's size 13, 6x sneakers again.

I was instructed by Rebecca to wear the boots at all times, not just at night, which I did. It was a very difficult time because it was a warm summer, and wearing the boots full time was very challenging. Due to the excessive swelling, I was very uncomfortable. I was also very depressed that all the hard work I had put into going to therapy, four times a week and all the wrapping, was for nothing.

By the time I got to see Rebecca again, I think she was surprised at how bad my feet and legs looked. Kathy had treated me initially when my extremities where that big after my hip surgery. We did, indeed, have to start over.

It didn't take long after initial therapy with Rebecca, that we were able to see progress. By the end of the treatment, I lost a minimum of two liters off of each leg. I felt like a different person. That awful discomfort that had been plaguing me for so long was gone.

I reapplied for another set of garments from the Marilyn Westbrook fund, and Rebecca and I decided on new garments called Juxta-Fit Day Time-Night Time Garments by Circaid. They worked like a dream.

Several months have passed and my feet and legs remain the size they were when I was discharged from therapy. Every night I wear my original Circaid Night Time Garments and in the morning change into the Juxta-Fit garments until I go to bed. I am so grateful to my Lymphedema Therapist, Rebecca, for her exceptional skill, compassion, and support. I am equally as grateful to the contributors of the Marilyn Westbook fund for their financial support, which has allowed me to reclaim my independence and sense of well being,

CHAPTER 21

The Edge

When a train goes through a tunnel and it gets dark, you don't throw
away the ticket and jump off. You sit still and trust the engineer.
—*Corrie Ten Boom*

Recently, I had an experience that pushed me over the edge, and plunged me into another sort of depression. I have been so used to having pain—the same pain—in my body. I also struggled with severe neck and shoulder pain. I got used to the spine issues. God was enabling me to manage all of it, although I struggled mightily with those terrible back spasms.

However, one day I woke up and the meaty part of my thumb hurt. *I mean, it REALLY hurt!* A few days later, the same thing happened to the thumb on my other hand. I was completely thrown by this. I made sounds like a whimpering puppy. I was not dealing with this latest physical problem as well as all the others, at all. It knocked the air right out of me.

I was surprised at my reaction to this new pain. Everything I did hurt. Even when I wasn't touching anything, my hand would throb. I lost the ability to concentrate, and found my coping skills were non-existent when dealing with new, terrible pain. I found myself getting angry, again. After several talks with God, I became embarrassed by my behavior. Here I was trying to deal with this situation by myself, again! It wasn't until I had laid this pain in my hands before the throne, that I got any relief. It showed me that relying on the Lord was not a one-time thing that would forever bring blanket coverage. Submitting myself to God is an ongoing process involving every situation, especially the ones that push you over the edge.

There was a lovely deaf woman, and mighty warrior for God, named Joanne, who was a beloved member of our local Deaf Christian Ministry. One day, she fell while outside and it resulted in a brain bleed. Joanne passed away one week later. I was asked to help interpret her funeral because there would be many deaf people in attendance. How could I do this? I couldn't even hold a book without getting severe spasms in my hands. It would be impossible. That night, I asked the Lord how I was going to do this. It was an honor to be asked to interpret for Joanne's service, but I did not think I was physically able. I considered canceling all together.

The morning of the funeral, I woke up with very little pain in my hands. I decided to go and help as much as I could. When I arrived, the other interpreters seemed very preoccupied with the upcoming responsibility of rendering an accurate interpretation of Joanne's funeral. I remember those planning meetings, and the binders full of information that we used to carry around in order to render a professional interpretation. I was not concerned about all that on that particular day. It had been so long since I had done this. The Lord blessed me with no pain in my hands at all, and clarity of mind to interpret! The Lord breathed upon me that day, and I was healed! It was a miracle! My spirit delighted in the Lord, and the presence of Holy Spirit, in that place, could be felt strongly by all who attended.

I had one of my greatest tests during the summer of 2010, when I had my gall bladder removed. I had been getting pain for a few weeks. Finally, my friends insisted that I make an emergency appointment for the next day, which I did. The doctor told me, over the phone, that he would send me directly to the hospital if the examination showed the results he suspected. The next morning I was very nauseous. I had a hard time driving to the appointment. I drove with my head out the window because I thought I would be sick. After the physical exam, it was determined that I should go right to the Emergency Room.

My cousin was away and I did not want to ruin her vacation. I could not seem to get anybody on the phone to go with me. I went alone. The next morning, the surgeon came into my room to tell me that I had an infected gall bladder and that it had to be removed that morning. Okay, I thought. So I called my friends and, still, nothing. The entire time, I found it so interesting that nobody was there for me.

Next, two women anesthesiologists came in my room to insert an intravenous line. They poked me with that thing, trying to find a vein, again and again and again. They tried different places in my arms, my neck, and my shoulder. At one point, I started crying. They asked if there was someone out in the waiting room that they could call for me. I cried like a child, with my lower lip sticking out and quivering, because I knew nobody was there waiting. After many more attempts to find a vein, I started screaming for them to get away from me. One woman said that I had to have the surgery because of the infection. Suddenly, I began to scream at the top of my lungs, on the inside,"JESSSUUUUSSSS HEEEEELLLLP MEEEEEEE!" I felt like again I was in an unending torture. This process was taking a really long time.

During this torture, I observed a man, dressed in medical scrubs and a surgical hat, walk by my door several times. He kept looking in at me. At one point, I saw him peek out of the door across the hall and stare at the group of us. All of a sudden, as if he couldn't take it anymore, this man rushed into the room and looked sternly at the anesthesiologists. They called him doctor somebody, and both snapped to attention as if they were in the army. This doctor instructed one of the women to get another intravenous needle ready. He started to speak to me and told me to relax. He took my hand ,and rubbed it, and told me it would be alright. It was as if this doctor was an angel straight from heaven sent just for me at that moment. He came out of nowhere, and proceeded to comfort me. He kept his eyes on me, and said that he was going to get the needle in my wrist and it would all be over in a minute. That needle went into my wrist, and I did not feel a thing. It took one second. I had shouted that silent scream for Jesus and my prayers were answered!

When I woke up from the surgery, nobody was there. I started to feel neglected. Where was everybody? Did they not care? I laid there and talked to the Lord. The comfort I received made me realize that I didn't need anybody else. Jesus was there for me, and that was all I needed. I never had that kind of experience before: Not being able to contact any of my friends or family for assistance. When it was time for me to be discharged, I had a hard time getting a ride home. My friend Tony drove over an hour to come pick me up, and take me home. I was so blessed. I realized that whatever happens to me, the Lord will always be there for me.

CHAPTER 22

Mourning

Elizabeth Kubler-Ross, in her book, *On Death & Dying*, published in 1969, uses the 'five stages of loss' to explain the emotions that a person dealing with grief may endure. The five stages are denial, anger, bargaining, depression and acceptance.

Thinking about what life used to be like before an illness can be daunting. The worst part is trying to lay to rest, the future you had imagined for yourself. It can really feel like a part of you died: your dream's demise.

I have observed many people go through the process. First, they insist nothing is wrong. Next, it is obvious that they are having physical difficulties, but they are "going to take care of it."

Some people have a temporary or acute illness, and their discomfort does dissipate over time with the proper medical attention. This doesn't happen for a person who has a chronic illness. Hold onto your hat, because that burst of anger is coming. After people realize that they have tried medication, physical therapy, surgery, and other treatments, and there is still little or no improvement in their condition, they experience overwhelming depression. Even the most mature Christians take a journey with the Lord down the road of despair. The realization that life has changed without our permission causes melancholy.

Why would God allow this? Fear and doubt, and even self loathing appear at a moment's notice. Instead of moving closer to the Lord, this is the time there are many lost to bitterness. This is a crucial fork in the road of your life. We all have options.

We can sit home, whine and pity ourselves, and make everyone around us miserable. We can become bitter, and helpless, and end up alone in a nursing home. But, I believe the best option is running into the arms of your Savior. Our King is intimately acquainted with our grief. He knows the number of hairs we have on our head. Luke 12:6-7 states, "Are not five sparrows sold for two pennies? Yet not one of them is forgotten by God. Indeed, the very hairs of your head are all numbered. Don't be afraid; you are worth more than many sparrows." His journey to the cross and his crucifixion was full of excruciating pain. He is no stranger to suffering and we are not strangers to Him. The Bible says that God does not want his children to suffer and it is His will that we be healed. Jeremiah 30:17 says. But I will restore you to health and heal your wounds,'declares the LORD, 'because you are called an outcast, Zion for whom no one cares.' We ask it in Jesus' name: *Please, Lord, heal me. Help me do your will. Give me back my strength, so I can serve you in a mighty way and glorify your name.* Sometimes, still nothing seems to change. The pain remains the same. The enemy would love to vex a seasoned Christian's soul by implanting the doubt that you are not worthy, whispering, "Your Lord does not love you". In John 8:44, Jesus proclaims (to the unbelieving Pharisees),"You belong to your father, the devil, and you want to carry out your father's desires. He was a murderer from the beginning, not holding to the truth, for there is no truth in him. When he lies, he speaks his native language, for he is a liar and the father of lies." We must not listen.

Why must we continually be in a condition of emptiness and totally naked before Him? Why is it important that we read and study scripture and pray without ceasing? The answer is simple, actually. The Lord is more concerned with our spiritual healing. He wants to send us the Holy Spirit to teach us, guide us, and help show us the way. He is glorified in our weakness. In 2 Corinthians 12:9, Paul demonstrates, "And He [Jesus] said to me, 'My grace is sufficient for you, for my power is made perfect in weakness.' Therefore, I will boast all the more gladly about my weaknesses, so that Christ's power may rest on me." The more we seek and obey Him, the more the true healing will happen: the healing of the spirit.

CHAPTER 23

ZZZZZZ *Chronic Fatigue* ZZZZZZ

Sleep is not my friend; it is my enemy. It steals time from my life. I sleep, on average, twelve hours per day. That is the norm when I'm not tired. When I'm tired, I can easily sleep through the entire weekend. I have called out of work, missed doctor's appointments, and numerous social engagements, because I was too exhausted to keep my eyes open. I even wrote a poem about my "Rod Iron Prison," which symbolized my bed. I often wondered if I would be able to get out of bed if my place caught on fire.

I went with a friend once to Myrtle Beach, South Carolina. She attempted to wake me up to no avail. Peg decided to go out for the day by herself. She returned to our hotel room around 4 pm. She said that I did not speak, but simply sat on the side of the bed. My friend watched me sleep sitting up for an hour. I remember hearing her come in and I thought, "This is our vacation, I have to get up!" But, I could only make it to the edge of the bed.

I always had trouble getting up for school as well. My mother told me that when I was an infant, she used to have to wake me up to feed me or I wouldn't eat! If I go to any social gatherings, I usually sleep though the next day. I used to joke about waking up at the, "crack of dinner." People's faces would wrinkle in disgust asking, "Oh, how can you stay in bed that long?" Believe me, it is not by choice. Sometimes, all I can manage is to get up just long enough to let my dog out, and feed him, on one of my "down under days." This kind of exhaustion can easily be brought on by one short outside activity.

Many people who suffer with a chronic disease have the opposite problem. They can't sleep because of the pain. The more restorative sleep missed, the more pain they are in. It is a vicious cycle that just keeps looping. The mind becomes cloudy, and the ability to make decisions becomes impaired as well. In my conversations with those people, with chronic pain that cannot sleep, they have explained how not sleeping can feel maddening. A person just wants to get a break from the pain, for even a short time to sleep, and yet they are kept awake because of it. Many people are expected to just pick up and carry on in the morning whether they have slept or not, because they either have small children or families.

CHAPTER 24

One Person Party

I should name this chapter of the book "Pity Party." Naturally, I'm the only one who shows up. This does not happen to me often at all, but, when it does, I throw lavish events!

My walker is so big and cumbersome. There is no hiding it or even minimizing it. Using my walker makes my obese buttocks stick up in the air for all to see how big it is. I guess there is no hiding that either. My gait is slow and unsteady. I often lose my balance, and if I didn't have the walker, I would fall. It isn't a pretty sight.

Recently, I decided that I was done with my walker. I did not want anything to do with it. I had convinced myself, you see, that I didn't really need it. *It's just that I have grown dependant on it*, I told myself. That walker was headed for the trash. I'm going to use my cane. *I'm SO done depending on that thing!*

One night, I was going to see my friend Eric play in his band. I decided to pick up my cane, and left my walker in the car. My friends came to the door to pick me up, and when I stepped outside, I almost fell on my face. It didn't take one minute to realize that I could not exist without my walker. Well, then I got mad. We walked and I teeter tottered to the car, and pulled out my walker. I kept raging in my mind, *What were you thinking?* The restaurant where the band was playing was very crowded. I had to walk in front of the band to get up several steps to the restroom. I felt like some kind of bizarre music video. People were really nice to me. They moved out of the way and tapped their friends on the shoulder to get them to clear a path for me as well. *Here comes mammoth Maureen with her mammoth walker and her mammoth behind stuck up in the air*, I thought they were thinking silently.

I am so sick and tired of every move being such an event. I can't go out without my wheelchair, so somebody has to push me around for the moment. If I take my shoe off because it hurts my foot, I have to ask somebody to put it back on for me. I GET TIRED OF IT!!!

I feel like just saying to God, *OK Lord that is enough! Please give me my old unobtrusive life back.* If only it was that easy. I do believe that God will help those who honor and obey Him; what I am feeling is irrelevant. This is God's world and He makes the decisions. Although I don't understand many things that happen, I know that God does. He sees the bigger picture.

Which makes me ask myself, *Where is all the thankfulness in this pity-party I have thrown for myself?*

Recently, I had a particularly hard night physically. I was very sore and tired, and transitioned into complain mode. I felt like I was going on, and on, about my physical limitations so much, that I actually got on my own nerves. As we were walking to my apartment, my friend Bryan said, "I don't know how you do it alone." I said it was God who helps me. It was the wisdom of my friend who said, "So you are not really alone." That was the right answer! I knew those words to be true.

I am never alone in this. Jesus knows what it feels like to be teaching his disciples one minute, and then, all of a sudden, chained and spat on. He knew it was God's will to experience all that, so he accepted it. I am glad that Jesus walks with me with each awkward and painful step because I know that I do not want to be alone in this. It would be too hard.

CHAPTER 25

Awkward Moments

Having chronic pain issues, and chronic illness, can cause many awkward moments. These are things that happen to many of us, and often cause us to stay home instead of taking a risk and traveling out of our comfort zone.

I bought a raised toilet seat to use for when I go visit my cousin's house. She has a small toilet that is low to the ground. It became increasingly difficult, as the months went on, to get up off of it. Instead of being stressed out during our yearly family gatherings, I decided to buy a raised toilet seat and leave it there.

Each time I went to my cousin's house, I would ask her where the toilet seat was, and she would always give the same answer, "In the basement." I thought since I had asked her many times, during different events, that she would remember I needed it during my visit over the holidays. When I arrived, there was no raised toilet seat to be seen, or found for that matter. I was livid. I wondered how she could just forget something that was so important to me. It is a necessity.

We all usually go to church together on New Years Eve. Last year, I had to drive home before meeting them at church to use the bathroom. This meant it was an extra trip in and out of the car, which is very difficult. I was so upset with what I perceived as a total lack of care for my needs, that I couldn't even concentrate on the service. When church was over, I marched over to another cousin and announced that if the toilet seat was NOT set up tomorrow, I was not coming for dinner. The next day, the toilet seat was there, and I could participate in the family dinner with no stress or worries.

109

I am appalled when people come to my house unannounced. On any given day, the sink can be full of dishes, stacks of clutter may be spread everywhere (my friend Eric calls it my Dr. Seuss piles), and piles of clean laundry may sit on my bedroom floor. Sometimes there is a bag of trash waiting to go out into the garbage can. I can only usually do one task per day. Sometimes I can't even manage that. This leaves me feeling humiliated when a casual acquaintance comes by. I wonder if I could be sued for death by cobwebs! I look forward to the times when my apartment is professionally cleaned.

My friends Jack and Gary have me over their house often for dinner. It is always a wonderful treat going there. I am treated like a queen, or a patron at a very elegant restaurant or fancy hotel. Gary is a great cook, and Jack provides all the humor one could ask for in an evening.

One time, during one of our dinners, we were sitting at the dinning room table. Everybody was talking, and laughing, and having a great time. Slowly, I felt excessive pain creeping over me. I stopped participating in the conversation. Suddenly, I felt like I was just going to burst out crying. I simply interrupted the dinner, and asked if I could please go lie down for a little while. Both Jack and Gary jumped up and escorted me to the bedroom on the lower level near the dinning room. I could tell by the looks on their faces that they were slightly confused, but more concerned than anything. It wasn't a terribly embarrassing moment, because we have been friends for many years, but it was an awkward moment, indeed. Needing a toilet seat, having a less than perfect apartment, and needing to rest in the middle of a dinner at a friend's house, are all situations that come arise when living with chronic pain.

I have great peace in knowing that God sees my struggles. He knows what I am going through. My Lord knows the pain I am in. I'm not bearing it alone. When the frustration mounts to where I can barely stand it, God is always there with His arms outstretched.

CHAPTER 26

Maureen and the Mermaid

For many years, I have been obsessed with mermaids. I collected mermaid posters, and books, and knickknacks. I have never quite understood why I have been so drawn to them. Recently, I realized that the mermaid represents everything I'm not: A symbol of fantasy, mermaids embody femininity, grace, and freedom. I was a girlie girl in the sense of the make-up, and the nail polish, but inside I never felt feminine. I preferred a leather jacket to your basic little black dress. I cannot have children, yet mermaids are a symbol of fertility. I also never had suitors lined up outside my door. Mermaids were beautiful sirens of the sea; they sit upon rocks and string pearls that they find on the ocean floor. They gather in their grottos, and comb their hair and make wreathes, and adorn themselves with flowers and shells and starfish. It is said that many a sailor has drowned, after jumping into the ocean, intoxicated by the beauty of a mermaid.

For a variety of reasons, I am very awkward. I am stiff and sore, and my movements are abrupt and rigid. Since I developed severe carpel tunnel, and other problems with my hands, I drop everything. I can't hold on to an eating utensil, food, paper—basically anything I can resemble the Three Stooges at times, but I'm alone. I'm frustrated to the point of tears on a daily basis due to my awkwardness.

Conversely, mermaids are so graceful, with the flowing hair and the beautiful movements, as they swim from shore to shore. Part woman and part fish, they glide peacefully and beautifully as they swim to their favorite rock to sing beautiful songs.

I am stuck in my body and held prisoner. My bed is my jailor. My wheelchair is a jail cell. My walker is like the wheel that prisoners use in other countries, where they walk around in a big circle for hours, going nowhere, for no reason. Mermaids symbolize freedom. They go to and fro, and travel the entire sea anytime they desire. The entire ocean is their play ground. They frolic in the moonlight with the other sea creatures. Mermaids rest on rocks and take refuge in caves. In reality, I don't sing any songs; I yell and I cry, and beg God for mercy. I am as cold and empty as any creature on the bottom of the ocean floor. I wish I had flippers as opposed to these hips that don't work, and a back that goes into spasm. A part of me wants to drift off into places unknown and glide along life like I used to.

CHAPTER 27

Inviting in a Vampire

As I understand folklore, a vampire cannot enter your home unless you invite him or her in. Sadly that is the truth when you are going through a crisis and are not familiar with the people who will be taking care of you. Those of us who would ordinarily have an eagle eye, in most situations, cannot recognize trouble when it walks through the door during a crisis. We are grateful for any help at all, and often overlook warning signs.

I would like to share two complete opposite experiences I had with two very different women: Samone, who lived with me in order to help me through a difficult time, and, Mary, who rented me an apartment.

Samone was a friend of my cousin's. Apparently, she was down on her luck, and was staying at my cousin's for a month. I paid her to clean, and cook, and help me around the apartment. She was very accommodating. We were both artists and could relate to each other on many levels.

When it was time to have my hip surgery, I asked Samone if she wanted to stay at my apartment and take care of Neelix while I was rehabilitating. She helped reorganize my apartment while I was gone. I felt like I had left my dog, and my home, in good hands. I was gone for three months, which was much longer than I had expected. During that time, Samone had settled in. She knew her way around the complex and the neighborhood, and became very comfortable in my apartment. She even managed to win the affections of my dog.

Things went well when I first came home. Samone was attentive; she took good care of me and the apartment, which was the agreement. Slowly, I started to see changes in Samone. She started to take long "walks" at all hours of the night. I could smell alcohol on her when she came in. She would tell elaborate stories about her journeys outside of the apartment. The trips became more frequent, and her absences would be longer. Then came a time when Samone lost all control. She brought strange men to the apartment. Additionally, she smoked cigarettes in the apartment when I had asked her not to, and began to carry on in a drunken stupor day and night. Eventually, I asked her to leave. She refused, saying that she had "established residency" and, sadly, the Collingswood Police agreed with her.

Living with Samone was very stressful. We argued regularly and the climate inside my own home was toxic. She lied, began to steal from me, and spent most of her time with her boyfriend that lived in the same building. As the months went on, the situation worsened. I realized that the only way I was going to get rid of Samone, was to move out. I was very leery of people after my experience with Samone. I just wanted to get as far away from that apartment complex as I could, so I wouldn't have to run into her again..

This brings me to Mary. The day I came to look at my current apartment, I met Mary and her husband, Mark. I was very nervous because, again, I had to deal with the Neelix factor. Neither of them flinched when discussing the fact that I had a dog, and that he was a pit-bull, which was a major relief. I remember Mary coming in to meet me and looking me straight in my eyes. I think she was checking me out that day.

It took me a long time to get acclimated to the new apartment—and the new town, for that matter. It was an area that I was not familiar with at all. I went from an apartment in a high-rise, where I could walk out my door and find somebody to chat with, to this place where I am isolated. I am also further away from my cousin and many friends.

Mary and I would greet each other and occasionally stop and talk, but I think that both of us needed there to be a line drawn between us. I was still recovering from my experience with Samone.

Four months after I moved in, I had an emergency gallbladder surgery. It was a very difficult time because I did not recover well or quickly. Mary was the first person at my door with food. She just didn't bring food once; she brought it for a week.

When I first moved in, the driveway was first come, first serve. There were six of us living in the same house. I started to notice that the driveway was always empty. I would see their cars parked on the road. I realized that they were leaving the driveway open for me. I was so touched and grateful.

In January, my rent check bounced. I was mortified. I only had a rent check bounce one other time in my entire life. Mary was very gracious, kind, and understanding. We worked out a payment strategy that worked for both of us.

Mary helps me out when I'm sick, tolerates Neelix's separation anxiety, and stays on top of the littlest thing I need as a tenant. She is not only my landlord, but a trusted and cherished friend. I couldn't be more blessed. I thank the Lord everyday for leading me to this family.

Often times, our family, friends, and neighbors keep their eyes out for us when we are not able. But, for every good story I hear about caregivers, I hear a bad one. It is a time when we are vulnerable, but still need to be vigilant.

CHAPTER 28

The Power of Pets

Pets provide much-needed company for folks that are isolated due to a chronic illness. The bond between people and their pets, might be what guards many from debilitating depression. Having the responsibility to care for a beloved furry friend, might be the very thing that gets some people out of bed. Animals provide joy, unconditional love, and moral support.

I went to a local "dog farm" in Mt. Laurel, New Jersey to look for a puppy the day I found Geordi. He was just a six week old black fur ball, with spots of white on his front paws and chest. Even as a small puppy, Geordi showed above-average intelligence. He would have been a perfect candidate for a therapy dog. The only thing that took some time: stopping Geordi from chewing the Bibles I had on bottom shelf of the bookcase. I loved to brag that Geordi was "Feasting on the Word." Geordi was very attached to me. He would follow me where ever I went in the house.

I have to say, Geordi was my true companion. He kept me company, stayed by me when I was sick, and comforted me when I was upset or sad. He was a very vocal dog. It was obvious when Geordi wasn't happy. He howled if he was upset, screamed if he was hurt, moaned if he was sick, and often insisted on the last word during an argument. I loved that about him. It was in that way, Geordi and I were very much alike. We never had to guess where the other one was coming from. We protected and understood each other.

I lost Geordi four months after my mother passed away. It was particularly devastating. Geordie died at home, with me sitting just several feet away. I still think I hear the sound of his collar when

BOUND BY ILLNESS, FREED BY GRACE

he walked around at night. Since Geordi was the alpha dog, Neelix was lost without him for quite a while. He has taken the brunt of all my emotional turmoil over the years. All the loss, the pain, and the physical trauma that has taken a toll on me, has also taken a toll on Neelix. He is a very nervous dog; he is literally afraid of his own shadow. I have some guilt associated with Neelix, and his lack of socialization, after he became older. I am not able to exercise him properly, which also contributes to his nervous condition. Neelix is not a complainer, unless I leave the house. Then he cries at the top of his lungs. Otherwise, he is very easily satisfied. He never complains and just aims to please. I have a harder time reading Neelix than I did with Geordi.

Neelix is the key to my past: I picked him out with Buck, my mother held him, he was around during all those dark days. He is the only living thing I see for days on end, at times. Often, I put my hand on him, as we settle down for the night, in order to feel his warmth. I smile during the night when I hear his snoring. Some mornings, I wake up and Neelix and I are wrapped around each other in the blankets. He sits up and looks like Darth Vader, until he gives me his best "Mother Theresa" (with the blankets still wrapped around his head.) He has always been my comic relief. Neelix loves the company of other humans. He is famous for his "drive-by" lickings. He stays in bed with me no matter how long I am there. He occasionally gets up to stretch or get a drink of water, but hops right back on the bed. On my bad days, I only get up to let Neelix out and feed him.

There is, unabashedly, a healing quality in our relationship with our pets. They accept and love us just the way we are, and simply want to please us. Our beloved animal friends are precious gifts from God.

CHAPTER 29

Disrespecting the Disabled

I often talk with other disabled folks when I see them out and about. I always find it so interesting to hear about the variety of perceptions and experiences that different people have. I have determined that a lot of what we perceive can be very telling.

My friend Mary Anne and I often talk about how kind people are, for the most part. I find this true in my personal experience. In a society where disabled people are marginalized, I am either too naive and/or oblivious to notice. Chronic pain has changed me, but to my knowledge, it has not changed who I am in the world. I just do things a little differently.

I have spoken to other people who have had the opposite experience. They find people to be cruel, and judgmental, when it comes to dealing with their pain. One woman categorized her immediate family in this category. She shared with me an experience she had when she was home alone. Apparently, she was in so much pain that she collapsed onto her kitchen floor. Upon her family's return, her husband and kids simply stepped over her while passing through the kitchen. This is an extreme example.

I believe that there are many other ways where people, who suffer chronic pain, can feel disrespected. One place can be at their doctor's office. There are some offices that are run so poorly, that a healthy person would get frustrated. They, often times, are not accommodating to the patient. Doctors, at times, can dismiss a person's pain as if it didn't exist, or accuse patients of lying to get pain medication.

I have been blessed with a sense of humor, a questioning mind, and a willingness to show my vulnerability. These three things have helped me navigate through even the most terrible of times, and many awkward situations. Sadly, I have also developed quite a temper, which tends to emerge when the sunny-side of my temperament is on vacation. This is usually on a day when my coping skills are low, and my frustration is high. I have noticed that when I am in the dark mood, most of the time, things move from bad to worse with lightening speed. It is during one of these moods where I can find fault with anybody over anything.

I received the local, town newspaper called, *The Legend*, and on the front page, I saw an advertisement for a local fitness center that was offering memberships for $10.00 per month. I decided to call and see if they had a warm-water therapy pool. They said, yes, and I was thrilled.

I went over to check out the facility before I joined. I was told that they had three pools. There was a huge lap pool where people swam laps, had family swims, and where swimming lessons were provided. There was another warm-water pool, which would be the one I would use with a depth of three to four feet. I was told that, at times, they would have lessons for groups of disabled folks, like Arthritis Classes and Physical Therapy. They informed me that I would not have to leave the pool if a warm-water exercise class was held. I was very excited about walking in the warm-water pool. I knew I would benefit a great deal from it.

The first time I went into the pool, I cried. The warm water rolling over my body was the most incredible feeling ever. I did not remember what it was like to be able to just walk. I would play like a kid in the pool, and practice walking different ways. I enjoyed the quietness; it was very peaceful. I would just circle the perimeter of the pool and talk to God. It was glorious. On occasion, I had to share the pool with other physical therapy patients. This was basically the way my visits went for the first six weeks.

One day, as I approached the pool, I could hear that there were children in the pool. I was NOT happy. I thought, *this has to end.* I had let it go once before, but I could not let this continue. I was not told that children would be using this pool, before I paid my money.

I approached one of the life guards. She agreed to ask the swimming instructor to get out of the pool. But, I told her that I would take care of it. The instructor was in the pool with the most beautiful little girl. Her parents were sitting on the bench right outside the pool. After their lesson, I walked into the pool room and tried to calmly ask the swimming instructor why she was using the warm-water pool instead of the lap pool for lessons. The woman looked at me askance, like I had two heads, and basically ignored me. I felt as though the swimming instructor, the life guards, and the facility as a whole, were very disrespectful to disabled people and their needs. They were ignoring policy by providing lessons to children in the warm-water therapy pool. *Why would people do that?* I felt that it was down right wrong.

I received a call from the facility manager. He told me that they always use that warm-water pool to give lessons to children. I told him that is not what I was told when I signed up, and that I thought it was a "bunch of crap," and that I was done with that place. It was not my finest hour. I was so angry about the entire situation. I felt like I was given the run-around. I never went back. It was just not a good situation for me. I have never been to a facility where the disabled folks shared a pool with infants.

※

Naturally, I have had some very "interesting" conversations with drivers on the Access Link Bus. One driver, referring to another driver, said, "Yeah, he thinks you are all stupid." In my humble opinion, even if that is true, it didn't need to be vocalized. I actually started laughing when I heard that. *Yep, I worked at a college for twenty years, gave presentations at national conferences, and co-developed an on-line notetaker training program that is used by Harvard, but I'm stupid because I'm in a wheelchair.*

I met another lady who said, "ahhh" (it was a pity ahhh), when I told her I lived alone. It was like she was surprised, or perhaps saddened by it. I had finally gotten a taste of feeling disrespected and belittled as a disabled person. In life, we all have bad encounters from time to time. The real test is how we respond to them.

CHAPTER 30

The What's Right Revolution

It doesn't matter on the level of pain, or an individual's pain threshold. Chronic pain inherently causes major frustration and a sense of desperation. There are times when we cannot see past the pain. For many of us, our entire lives revolve around our chronic illness, and it is hard to think of anything else. The reality is that there are other things existing around us, in addition to the prison of pain that we find ourselves entrapped in. We haven't fallen out of love with the same things that used to bring us joy and satisfaction. Those things are still there. We just lose our focus.

In a society of people always asking each other, "What's wrong?" I am challenging you to ask yourself, "What's right?" We already know the answer to what's wrong: we hurt, often badly. Now, it is difficult to find anything that might appear right. Recently, I was asked to run a Bible study for our Deaf Ministry's Thanksgiving Celebration. I was planning a group activity: to ask the members to write five things they were grateful for. I sat down to construct my own list, and I was coming up blank. I couldn't believe it. I see myself as a fairly positive person, but I was struggling. Was I getting so consumed by the pain, that I stopped seeing all of the Lord's blessings? I decided to think about the things that I enjoy. The list is as follows: The laughter of children, a watermelon Yankee Candle, George Winston's music, worshipping God, joking with friends, the smell of fresh sheets, the feel of my favorite blanket, prayers that are answered, Buster Keaton and Charlie Chaplin movies, hazelnut coffee, candlelight, sharing what the Lord is doing, holidays with my family, baby animals, the color of autumn leaves, Christmas carols, Tiffany lamps, meeting new people, talking to old friends, reading books, snowfall, a good thunder and lightening storm, Celtic music, looking through old pictures, watching fish swim in an aquarium, art, foreign movies, hearing the Holy Spirit and obeying, crab cakes etc. The list could go on to infinitum.

The interesting thing about that list is that there are things I can still enjoy and do. Those are things that I have always enjoyed. Now that my chronic pain has moved in, it doesn't mean that I can't enjoy anything anymore. All these things I can still enjoy from my recliner or my bed. It is just a little harder to concentrate on what's right. What's right with you today?

Are God's promises written on your list of things that are right with you today? They should be. Here are several of our God's promises:

"Come to me, all you who are weary and burdened, and I will give you rest."
-Matthew 11:28

"My God will meet all your needs according to His glorious riches in Jesus Christ."
-Philippians 4:19

"I will refresh the weary and satisfy the faint."
-Jeremiah 31:25

"I have told you these things, so that in me you may have peace. In this world you will have trouble. But take heart! I have overcome the world."
-John 16:33

"For He will deliver the needy who cry out, the afflicted who have no one to help."
-Psalm 72:12

"All the prophets testify about Him that everyone who believes in Him receives forgiveness of sins through his name."
-Acts 10:43

"If you forgive men when they sin against you, your heavenly Father will also forgive you."
-Matthew 6:14

CHAPTER 31

We Are At War

As followers of Christ, we often suffer. Not because we are out of God's will, but because we are in it. Not because we lack faith, but because we have faith. We suffer, not because we need to be filled with the Spirit, but, because we already are. Stronger faith does not mean less suffering, but more suffering means stronger faith. Far from calling our faith into question, our afflictions result in our becoming more and more like Christ Himself. —D.R. McConnell

Satan's biggest achievement is to cause so much havoc in the life of a Christian, that he or she will take his or her eyes off of the Lord. Pain certainly causes chaos, and a lot of it. The enemy will just bide his time, and keep pressing us in our weakest areas. We all know that chronic pain can cause relentless pressure on the patient, and the family unit. Chronic suffering can cause spiritual doubt, and a loss of confidence, especially when we compare ourselves to our able-bodied counter parts, and stop thinking about how God sees us. Suddenly, we start to focus on our limitations rather than our strengths. We forfeit the joy of the riches we have been promised in Jesus Christ.

What happens if we stop looking to the Lord, and buckle under the pressure of Satan's attacks? Little by little our faith starts to dwindle, and sin starts to take over our lives. It can begin as a simple thought. "God doesn't care about me. He wouldn't allow me to go through this." The Liar can whisper this dark and negative message, which can wind up permeating our souls if we are not careful.

Why would the devil delight in a Christian's despair? One less

Christian witnessing for God, is one more seeming victory for him. If Satan can fool a spiritual light into believing it has been extinguished, he will. That is his full-time job. If a Christian plunges back into his/her former way of life, the Enemy believes he has won. Once a brother or sister in Christ abandons his, or her, relationship with Jesus, that is one less person sharing the Gospel. What looks like a ruined testimony, is the outcome of spiritual warfare. Our hearts and minds must dwell on the truths of the Lord in order to maintain our spiritual integrity.

In Romans 8:26, the author suggests, "In the same way, the Spirit helps us in our weakness. We do not know what we ought to pray for, but the Spirit himself intercedes for us through wordless groans." Oddly enough, sometimes it feels like we are fighting the church. So many people have turned from God, and left the church, due to teaching that suggests that s the person suffering is responsible for not receiving the healing he or she seeks. Either there is unconfessed sin, or a lack of belief, or a spiritual weakness. Somehow we are just not "good enough." That adds insult to injury. Is that not further oppressing the oppressed? Where is God in that equation? Isn't it up to God when and how people are healed? Since Jesus' death of the cross, when have we had to be "good enough?"

We don't choose how God is going to heal us. We choose how we are going to cope with our present circumstances. Will we get angry and turn away from God? Will we just decide to simply exist, and allow our lives to count for nothing. Are we going to accept Satan's lies, that we are useless spiritually because we must have angered God in some way to wind up in this situation? How will you choose to survive your suffering?

Initially, I tried to go it alone, and take care of things my own way. I suppose I thought that I could do a better job than God. I quickly saw that it wasn't working. After a brief temper tantrum, I realized that there was only one way; and that way was to submit to the Lord. Through continual prayer, studying the Word, and listening to the leading of the Comforter, God gives me the strength to stay in this battle. I now know that, in order to have any quality of life, I must be rooted in Jesus Christ. God can reach beyond my pain, and love me though my suffering. My soul echoes agreement with Hebrews 11:25, "He chose to be mistreated along with the people of God rather than to enjoy the fleeting pleasures of sin."

CHAPTER 32

No Mo Mojo

Prayer is exhaling the spirit of man
and inhaling the Spirit of God. —Edith Keith

I spent a lifetime building a persona to hide behind. I cultivated it and nurtured it, and it became a way to seemingly protect myself from the outside, and inside, world. I used it as a shield and a natural barrier, but ultimately, it became a spiritual prison.

Years ago, I appeared to be a very trendy lady who had a cool edge to her. I wore leather, had multiple tattoos, and attended annual biker rallies. I had a unique style. I was a very creative person. I loved all the arts, especially the visual arts. I loved going to bookstores, and collecting books. I enjoyed creative writing and foreign movies. I also loved learning about other cultures. I was constantly on the go. I went to nice restaurants, and drank imported wine. I loved going out to a bar to listen to mostly blues, or rock and roll. I had a wild side, for sure. I had a successful career. I worked for twenty years at a local community college's, Center for Students Who Are Deaf and Hard of Hearing. I loved my job at the college. It was difficult and stress-ful, but well worth the time and the effort. I loved the students, my colleagues, and the other faculty members who I worked with there. Life was good.

I had a very private relationship with the Lord. I knew that my behavior was neither that of a faithful believer, or a child of God. I don't think I had a notion of what God's grace meant, or who God really was. I didn't understand God's love. The Lord was always with me, and that I always knew. I went through a time when I read the Bible, and prayed regularly, and sought the Holy Spirit. Other times I cursed like a sailor, and had major anger issues. When I got mad, all my colleagues would run away from me which always made me terribly sad.

I smoked, I drank alcohol, and I spent money recklessly. I ate whatever I wanted, and as much as I wanted, and gave no respect to the body God gave me.

My disability took everything away. My position as a college administrator was the first thing to go. I pushed myself so hard, for so long, that I seemed to have fallen apart overnight. It was quite obvious to everyone that I had been struggling for several years, physically, before I could no longer work.

The cruelest thing that was taken away from me was my self-perceived mojo. I have paraded around and flashed this character for the world to see since High School. That was my hiding place, my total comfort zone, and the essence of who I thought I was.

Suddenly, I couldn't walk, and when I did, it was with great difficulty. I had no time or inclination to worry about my "style." No more ornamentation. The clothes, make-up, and jewelry no longer mattered. I didn't care about foreign movies, or art, or music. The tattoos that danced on my chest mocked me, because they were a reminder of my former self. Every passion I had suddenly dissolved and the world lost its color. I had a new self. Actually, I would not call it the makings of a person at all. This newly disabled Maureen stayed in a bed, a heap of blubber, not knowing what to do. Suddenly, "Miss Bossy Cool Pants" had no control over anything. In fact, I could barely move. There was nobody around to tell me that I was awesome. I didn't brush my hair or shower. Everything that made me the person I thought I was, had vanished. What do I do now, I wondered?

It wasn't until God had purged me of that person, that He could make me a new creation. God loved me so much, that he allowed me to fall down so He could bring me up. I had to be in this weakened state, both physically and spiritually, to be molded in the image of God. I had to know this suffering to be able to know God's grace.

People often ask me if I get mad at God for allowing all the sickness and pain. "Yes," I answer, "I used to." Now I thank Him everyday for it. It is the Lord's cleansing fire for my soul. It took all of this for me to understand that none of this is about me. Everything is about glorifying God. I feel so blessed to know this sacred truth.

When my feet and legs are swollen, or I am having back spasms, or my rotator cuff is causing me pain, or the callous on the bone of my foot is hurting me, I turn to Him. Once you have lost everything, you are free to do anything.

The Book of Psalms, Chapter 30:2, states, "LORD my God, I called to you for help, and you healed me." There are many forms of healing. The Lord heals my soul, which is where I need it the most, and I praise Him for that. If God simply healed my body, it would be easy to forget about His miracles like the Israelites did after they fled Egypt. Although God obviously has the power to heal me, He may choose not to. The reason is known only to God. I might have something to learn or some comfort to give to others. The Lord has given me work to do.

One day, as I was studying the bible in the book of Job, a verse almost went by un-noticed. My eyes saw it, and when I processed the magnitude of the lesson, I was amazed. In the prior verses, Job was informed about the loss of his children and all his possessions. In Chapter 1, verse 20, it says, "At this, Job got up and tore his robe and shaved his head. Then he fell to the ground in worship." Job worshipped. Job lost everything and he worshipped! What a lesson that is. When troubles come, the first thing I do is complain and groan, and ask God to take care of it. Job's response would classify as insanity by today's standards.

I never thought of praising God immediately, until I really studied the Book of Job. That was the first thing Job did; he went to the Lord. He did not yell, ask why, or demand answers. He simply worshipped the Lord. That is such a powerful message to all of us who have crisis in our lives.

The Book of Job teaches us many lessons. My favorite scripture in the Bible is Job 1:21: "Naked I came from my mother's womb, and naked I will depart.[a] The LORD gave and the LORD has taken away; may the name of the LORD be praised." There we see it again. Job just lost everything—his family, his possessions, his health—but he gives God glory.

I love Job's reasoning: We come into the world with nothing and we leave with nothing except what the Lord has for us at that time. The one constant thing is that God loves us during the good and bad times. In Job, 2:10, the author demonstrates, "Shall we indeed accept good from God and not accept adversity? In all this Job did not sin." Job did not sin. God was pleased with Job.

CHAPTER 33

My Testimony

God intended something beautiful in my brokenness, although it may remain hidden to those who cannot see with a mystical vision. My broken body may have little worth to our culture, but it has remarkable value to God. My brokenness gives me insight into true reality, and it is a window into my being. Through it I've found the wellspring of God's love that lives deep in my soul and my own hidden wholeness.
—*Diana Ventura*

For most of my adult life, between my pride and spiritual ignorance, I shut Jesus out. I didn't really need to bother Him, because I believed that I had things under control. I did pray often for others and myself. I also depended on the prayers of others. I figured if He didn't want to listen to me, He would surely listen to somebody who I perceived as being closer to Him. It didn't matter who prayed, just as long as they did it. I wasn't in God's good graces, so I dare not attempt to pray myself without help. I was the one who would do the fixing, though, because I knew better. Or, so I thought.

I always knew the Lord was there working in my life, and controlling the world that He made. I had reverence for Him as well. What I did not have was a healthy fear of God. I casually asked for forgiveness when it crossed my mind. *Oh well, I was weak. The spirit is willing, but the flesh is weak. Yep, that was me. If the Apostle Paul felt that way, then I presumed it applied to me too. God knows the deal.*

I did not understand what a relationship with Jesus really meant.

I knew he died on Calvary for my sins, and that I would be going to Heaven because of that act on His part. I loved going to church and learning more about His word. I was fine as long as nothing was asked of me. I avoided Bible studies or other ministries. I struggled to make connections with other people at church. I did not feel comfortable in my own skin around other Christians, and I could not understand why. Often times, maintaining eye contact was a struggle.

I had a difficult life growing up, and have been through two difficult marriages. My life did not reflect the joy and peace that I saw in the lives of other Christians that attended church. I couldn't understand what I was doing wrong. I believed that Jesus was God's son and that he died for my sins, and I awaited His return. What was missing?

Remember, within a space of three years, I had lost my marriage, my home, my beloved mother, my career of twenty years, my dearest dog, and, finally, my health and all my finances. I was beyond distraught and very angry at God. I didn't get it. I wondered what I had done that was so bad to cause all these terrible things to happen to me. I had been so blessed for so long, but suddenly everything was stripped away from me.

It was during this time that I laid my face down before the Lord. I started to talk to Him, daily. I would call upon His name literally, each time I took one step. Everything changed when I decided to seek God's face, and pray, which produced transformation. It was then that the Lord pierced my soul, and showed me His mercy. I had a spiritual awakening. The Holy Spirit was there giving me comfort, strength, and direction.

I began to form a very strong relationship with God through my illness. To the outside world, it might sound like madness to say that I was glad the Lord allowed me to go through all these trials, especially the chronic pain. I finally experienced what it means to know God's power, after I started to read God's Word and pray continuously. I became filled with the peace, and acceptance and, yes, joy.

My health improved slightly, but my soul slowly became whole.

God continues to bless me daily and teach me more about who He is. I am glad for every pain and uncomfortable feeling, I have had and will have. It is what reminds me of God's love for me, and that I am a child of God. It reminds me of what Christ went through on the cross. I eagerly await His return, so I can inherit a heavenly body. My life has really changed. My days were once filled with unbearable pain, loneliness, and deep depression. The pain is still there, and things are far from perfect, but thanks to the Holy Spirit, my spirit can soar beyond it with hope.

Afterword

When my lease was up in the high-rise complex, I found a mother-in-law suite in a nice neighborhood. My landlords live above me and are attentive to my needs. I have no stairs to climb. The access into my apartment is more than accommodating. Neelix has a leash attached to the house so that I can just let him out; he doesn't need to be walked.

For a very long time, I prayed to find a church home. An old friend, Julie, would drive forty-five minutes one-way to pick me up and take me to her church every Sunday. She only lived five minutes away from her church. The church, Victory Assembly of God, was wonderful. The Pastor, and his wife, had a heart for the growing Deaf Ministry.

During my involvement with that ministry, I saw miracles happen. The numbers of deaf folks attending the church grew by leaps and bounds. I witnessed the deaf congregation become an equal and important part of the church. It was amazing. I wanted more.

I wanted to go to Bible Study, join other ministries, learn and grow with my church family, but that was very difficult because of the distance. It became apparent that I would need to find a church that was closer. I prayed for God's guidance.

One day, my friend Jennifer mentioned a church that I used to pass frequently when I lived in my former apartment, Oaklyn Baptist Church. The initial draw was that they had an elevator, and I could attend all of the services and activities. Essentially, the church was handicapped friendly. Even more, the church was interested in working with me to establish a ministry for women suffering with chronic illnesses. It didn't take long before I knew that this was the church the Lord was leading me to.

In the beginning, I had to force myself to attend activities. Now it comes naturally. I attended the "Inquiry Class" and later became a member. I unknowingly joined a book club that sends me different books every month. These help me grow spiritually as well. I still attend the Deaf Ministry bible study, held every other Friday night, taught by my very own friend, Julie Doerrmann.

It was this group of amazing deaf folks that loved me back to health. I could see that God was taking care of me both spiritually and physically. God led me to find a scholarship, from the Marilyn Westbrook Fund, to purchase the Circaid boots I needed to control my Lymphedema. I called about a power wheelchair, and five days later there was one resting neatly in my kitchen. I could go on and on, I could speak forever of the wonderful blessings the Lord has bestowed upon me: I went back to Virtua in Motion Rehabilitation Department—for physical therapy—for my hands. Additionally, I received a free month-membership in a local fitness center with a warm-water therapy pool; the employees respect disabled people and go out of their way to assist them.

I have come to cherish my time alone with God. I love worshipping Him. I love allowing him to be in control of my life. The Holy Spirit comforts me and leads me to every destination, if I listen. My life is not perfect, and my flaws are many, but I know I am forgiven because of what Jesus did on the cross. God gives me the strength to deal with the pain.

Episodes of acute pain keep me vigilant, and chronic pain keeps me humble. Pain is unforgiving. The good news: my Lord is forgiving. Without God, I would have never survived any of it.

Admittedly, childhood dreams and heartbreaks still follow me: I will remember the sound of my mother's voice as she sang to me—sweet little South African Children's songs—as a child. I will remember the fragrant smell of my father's pipe—soft notes of cherry tobacco—that filled the house on Sunday afternoons, the sultry music of Connie Francis and Edith Piaf, the bellowing laughter from the living room as my father and I watched our favorite British show. I will remember the midnight stirrings—the marital madness—the distant echoes of raised voices and harsh words. But, most of all,

I will remember the laughter.

About the Author

Maureen Brady grew up in Lindenwold, New Jersey. Maureen's childhood interest in American Sign Language developed into life long career as a Sign Language Interpreter. In 1988, Maureen was hired at Camden County College, in Blackwood, NJ, at the Mid Atlantic Post-Secondary Center for Students who are Deaf or Hard of Hearing. However, in 2008, her health declined to the point that Ms. Brady could no longer maintain her successful career.

Maureen currently resides in Cherry Hill, NJ with her one-year-old, blind cat, Hash. She is the creator of the "Whats Right Revelation," an online site dedicated to encouraging people with chronic pain by use of Scripture & daily thanksgiving posts. Maureen is active in a number of on line support groups as well as an active member of Oaklyn Baptist Church in Oaklyn, NJ.

mobrady210@gmail.com

Made in the USA
Charleston, SC
09 February 2014